YOUR
HOW TO ACCEPT THE ANSWERS
JOURNEY
YOU DISCOVER
TO
ALONG THE WAY
SUCCESS

YOUR JOURNEY TO SUCCESS

HOW TO ACCEPT THE ANSWERS YOU DISCOVER ALONG THE WAY

KENNY WEISS

Copyright ©2018 by Olicartin, LLC
All rights reserved.

Published in the United States.

ISBN: 978-1-98147-101-0

Disclaimer: While all stories in this book are true, some names and identifying information have been changed to protect the privacy of the individuals involved. This publication is not intended as a substitute for professional medical or mental health advice, diagnosis, or treatment. The author makes no warranty, guarantee, or promise, express or implied, regarding the effectiveness of this material. What you are about to read can invoke some strong feelings you've been attempting to avoid for a long time. To soften the blow, I will share examples from my own train wreck of a life to show you how anybody can do this. As you begin examining your own life, a natural reaction to these strong feelings is to deny them. That's exactly what I am challenging you *not* to do.

You will learn how society and your brain and body are all set up to further your denial and keep you from what you want. The good news is I will describe concrete ways to overcome that natural reaction. If you are willing to do the work required, what you experience will be life changing. But the caveat is that you need to do the work. Be gentle with yourself. Maybe you won't feel ready to do some of your journey to success steps when you reach them at the end of each chapter. That is okay; these steps require personal reflection. During periods of my life, I wasn't ready to either. That doesn't make you "bad." Know that what you are about to embark on is a lifelong process and that this process doesn't require perfection. For some, reading the book through in its entirety and then revisiting sections and completing the action steps at the conclusion of each chapter is ideal. Do what works best for you, knowing I'm with you every step of the way.

DEDICATION

To my parents, for all the ways they loved me perfectly and imperfectly. I needed both to find me.

To my brothers and sister, for your constant forgiveness and acceptance of me.

To my children, for if it wasn't for them I would not be here.

To the two women who married me. For who I was at the time, you loved me exactly as I wanted and needed to be loved. You never failed me.

To my counselor Mike Pinkston, who saw in me what I could not see in myself and who gave me the tools to find it.

To Andy Freeman, for never leaving and giving me the insight as to what fear really is.

To my clients, who were brave and willing to help others by sharing their journey through the Worst Day Cycle so that others could as well.

To me, for my courage to expose the truth, the darkness of who I am including the good, bad, and especially the ugly. For constantly pursuing answers as to why I have been in so much pain and so hurtful to others but, most of all, to myself. If I had not been willing to expose to myself how traumatized, afraid, and shameful I felt and how judgmental, narcissistic, and soul-suckingly manipulative I can be, I would not have ever discovered the answer to finding peace, self-acceptance, and true success. It is because of that courage I have learned that my light, my greatness, everyone's greatness, is in the one place we have all wrongly been conditioned and told to avoid. Just like a sunrise, our darkness gives birth to our light.

ACKNOWLEDGMENTS

I would like to acknowledge those who have helped me create and propel my theory of the Worst Day Cycle.

Mike Pinkston—My counselor taught me how to be a man and coach others. Every single day of my life his words, counseling style, and wisdom flow from me. As I grow, I gain a deeper insight into what he was teaching me. They're little nuggets of new growth waiting for me as my knowledge and self-awareness increase.

Andy Freeman—While going through my second divorce, Andy gave me the definition for fear that I use with all my clients. It changed my life.

Bessel Van der Kolk—I learned that it is universal how trauma runs everyone's life.

Brené Brown—I discovered the destructiveness of shame and the necessity for vulnerability.

Byron Katie—She taught me how we live in the opposite and how denial is rampant in us all and, I believe, it is the single greatest killer in our society.

Candace Pert—She scientifically confirmed something I intrinsically felt—that everything we do is based on feelings, that almost all health issues are feelings based, and that science knows this and disregards it.

Eckhart Tolle—He enlightened me on how to be present in each moment.

Joe Dispenza—He furthered my understanding of how trauma is universal in us all, that it is passed down through generations, that the brain and body store it, and that our health is a direct result of this carried trauma.

Louise Hay—She taught me self-love and self-esteem. Her books should be mandatory reading for all ninth graders.

Pia Mellody—She taught me that what we all consider to be love is incorrect—how we are all love addicted, love avoidant, and codependent. It could be no other way because it is all we have ever seen modeled. Her books should be mandatory reading for all high school seniors.

Tony Robbins—He taught me how to set up a structure/process for change.

ABOUT THE AUTHOR

Kenny Weiss is a coach and speaker at the forefront of the personal development field. Through his own personal journey and nearly thirty years of studying about the role emotions play in our lives, he brings a one-of-a-kind skill set to individuals, families, and businesses that are looking for more happiness and success personally and professionally.

Kenny's journey included multiple addictions, two divorces, a bankruptcy, playing two professional sports he never wanted to play, and contemplating suicide. In other words, he has not only studied the process, he has lived it and overcome it. Kenny's clients include successful entrepreneurs, professional athletes, individuals, and families who have discovered what current science now tells us—emotions are at the center of everything we do. If any area of your life isn't producing the results you know you are capable of, Kenny has the knowledge and experience to get you back on track.

CONTENTS

Introduction | 1

Chapter 1: The Day Everything Changed | 7

Chapter 2: The Mind-Body Connection | 15

Chapter 3: Trauma = Loss of Connection | 25

Chapter 4: How Our Parents Traumatize Us | 33

Chapter 5: White-Hot Fear | 53

Chapter 6: Shame: The Silent Epidemic | 67

Chapter 7: The Trap of Denical | 79

Chapter 8: The Day I Saw My Darkness | 93

Chapter 9: The Power of Saying No | 101

Chapter 10: Are You the Hostage or Hero in Your Career? | 113

Chapter 11: The "Let It Come" Approach | 121

Chapter 12: The Beginning of a New Journey | 129

Appendix: Your Journey to Success Toolkit | 135

INTRODUCTION

As a life coach, I show people how to live in the best day of their lives. Imagine what it would be like to wake up each morning knowing that whatever comes your way, you will have what it takes to make it your best day. I help people identify and remove the obstacles that prevent them from achieving that vision.

We have all started or ended our day thinking about what we should have done in our personal or professional lives to attain our goals. But, somehow, we couldn't seem to get ourselves to do it. As we lie there and consider the steps it would take to realize our dreams, there was a feeling we couldn't overcome. That feeling is what kept us from pursuing what we wanted—it stopped us from taking action. We have read books on how to make our careers and relationships better, but we are still stuck. None of the other wonderful success processes in those books can be fully implemented until this work is done—until we can find a way to move beyond this feeling. This book bridges that gap and offers sound information to help us understand why we are inexplicably stalled in our endeavors. It then offers tried-and-true strategies to help us finally let go of that feeling and fully go after our dreams.

The Worst Day versus the Best Day Conundrum

My theory on why we are stuck is based upon what I call the Worst Day Cycle. Getting out of it requires a shift into our best day. To jump-start this process, ask yourself the following:

1. **Do you remember the best day of your life?** Take some time here. What happened on this day? A best day might be when you felt at peace with yourself and you liked who you were in that moment. It doesn't need to be a momentous occasion like a birth of your child or your wedding day. Think of it as an ordinary experience where a certain feeling overcomes you, like when you witness an athlete being in the zone. At that point, they are living a moment without judgment or self-criticism. Our best day is unencumbered by shame and denial. Instead, we are feeling pure joy, clarity, and spontaneity.

2. **What was the worst day of your life?** Can you see it, smell it, hear it? Do tears well up in your eyes or do you get a lump in your throat? Does your heart ache? Does your stomach flip or other parts of your body hurt as you relive that moment that marked your worst day?

When I asked what the best day of your life looked like, did you struggle? Or did you think of some so-so days or maybe a good day, but you didn't instantly think, feel, and picture a life-changing incredible moment that gave you shivers? Was it hard for you to even come up with one? When I ask the best day question during a presentation, invariably only about one out of forty people raise their hand with a response. Usually those who do just describe an event with very little emotion or satisfaction. That's because they are stuck in their worst day and can't feel real joy because of it. When a so-called best day happens, the remnants of the worst day overpower it. When I ask about the worst day, the room goes heavy and dark with emotion. People's faces and gaze drop, they shift in their seats, they go blank and numb and stare off into space as they relive the feeling of that worst day.

Stuck in That Worst Day

Nearly all of us are stuck in the worst day of our life. The trauma from that day is where that feeling comes from and it is the birthplace of the Worst Day Cycle. Since there is no mechanism in place for overcoming trauma, this cycle is the natural maladaptive coping skill we use to survive it. While it is effective in the short-term in that it keeps us alive, in the long-term this cycle ultimately works against us and over time kills us and our dreams. The cycle compounds with time because we re-inflict the trauma from that day on ourselves. We are continually gaining new layers and more pain as it becomes further entrenched in us.

We are all reliving our worst day on a daily basis. It is why we can't find peace and success. I'm not talking about what we all think of as success, such as the acquiring of things or status. Cars, houses, the trophy spouse, the office in the corner... all those "things." Most of us who have achieved this type of "success" are more miserable and numb inside because we have chased those things hoping they would take away that feeling only to find out that they don't. Don't misunderstand me; I am a proponent of having nice things. What I am saying is that we achieve true success when we like who we are, feel at peace, and accept ourselves and when we feel all of that whether or not we have acquired those other things in life. No matter where we are in our life process, that worst day feeling shouldn't have the power to jump up and stop us.

New Information Requires a New Mindset

If at any time you feel any sort of negative feeling or think negatively about yourself while reading this book, you need to know that comes from your Worst Day Cycle. I want to make this clear: you aren't bad and you aren't incapable. You just have never been given the information to escape this cycle. We can only do what we know. You can't overcome something you weren't even aware was operating in you. Sometimes you are going to want to put this book down, as you won't want to go where I am taking you. That feeling will come up and it may be too difficult to face. That is fine; that is normal. If you discover that your trauma is triggering you, talk to a helping professional. It's okay to take breaks, but realize you need to acclimate your brain. The more you familiarize yourself with the content, the better you'll be able to understand and apply it to your life.

The Incredible Value of Doing the Work

Why do all this hard work? There's a reason. My client shared the following:

The day I walked into Kenny's office for the first time, I was at the end of my rope. I sat slumped over in my chair barely able to take a breath as I held back my tears. I remember feeling completely lost, hopeless, and had zero sense of self-worth—the result of a lifetime of saying yes to everyone but myself.

At this point in my life, I was quickly climbing the career ladder within my industry and had a job that paid great. I was expecting to become engaged to someone I deeply cared for within the year, and I had two parents who adored me and supported me in every way possible. My life was perfect by society's standards, yet I would lie awake every night dreading having to wake up the next day. The reality was that I was living in a complete delusion, had zero boundaries, and was unable to identify my own wants and needs, let alone meet them. Remember that great job I was talking about? That perfect relationship? My nurturing family? It was all a fantasy. I (a person with no boundaries) was surrounded by other people with no boundaries, all of whom exploited one another's lack of boundaries.

With Kenny's guidance, I quickly became aware of how deeply entrenched I was in codependence and self-victimization. I saw it as a generational pattern and a pattern that I was continuing within my own life and relationships. As I began setting healthy boundaries and experiencing healthy levels of self-esteem, my life changed drastically. I lost friends, quit my job, and was finally able to leave a three-year love-ad-

dicted relationship. All of this happened in a matter of weeks. The old me would've completely shut down in this situation. I would've spent months feeling sorry for myself and self-medicating in various ways just to make it through the day. This time was different. I now viewed these circumstances as an opportunity to finally create the life that I wanted, not the life that other people wanted for me.

Your Journey Awaits

We all want to avoid the darkness that lies in the unknown. By going on this journey, you will gain the tools and understanding you never had. Use those tools to leave the darkness of that worst day, step into your greatness of that best day, and overcome your fear of success. You are great, incredibly great, but you have never been given these essential tools to be great or to succeed… until now. Your greatness awaits you on the other side.

Chapter One
The Day Everything Changed

It was the middle of the night and the house was pitch black. I stumbled down the hallway using my hands to feel the walls because turning on lights in the middle of the night was not acceptable. I knew the walk well. I had navigated it many times in the dark. My small hand found the familiar trim and case molding of the doorjamb to the bathroom. Because closing the door in a normal way could instigate a thunderous reprimand, I had a method to avoid making any noise. With one hand on the doorknob, I would slowly and silently turn the knob so the bolt was inside the door. To avoid any creaking in the door hinges, I would use the other hand to apply pressure against the door, stiffening the hinges, taking out any slack and therefore any noise. The door-closing process could take between ten and fifteen seconds.

Once the door was closed without incident, a sense of relief washed over me. The most treacherous part of using the bathroom at night was over. Or so I thought. As I tiptoed toward the toilet, I was still in the dark in the outer vanity area because even the light coming from under the door could cause problems with my parents. I had to wait until I got to the water closet to turn on the light. My left hand located the doorjamb. Just inside on the wall at about chest height I found the light switch and flipped it on. I froze. There was my mother, passed out naked on the toilet.

Immediately, I felt a rush beginning in my feet, an electrical warmth filling both legs simultaneously. Envision something like the old *Star Trek* show when they were transported out of the USS Enterprise. As the rush accelerated and began to overtake me, I heard myself screaming inside, "I'm changing, I'm changing." I instinctively knew that who I was up until that moment at age ten was leaving me. I would never be that person again. The "I" or "me" that I knew was dying and I could do nothing to stop it. Just before the final surge of electricity swept over me, the completion of my previous life, I tried to shake my mom awake. I attempted to sit her up and begged her to speak to me. That's when the tears started to cascade down my face and the panic set in, "Mom, please don't be dead. Please Mom, wake up."

I have no memory of what happened next. I felt as if I were transported out of my body like Captain Kirk and Mr. Spock being beamed to an alien planet. I had to separate from this moment before I could be put back together and go to another place. My next memory is being on the couch in the family room cradled in my dad's arms. My head is buried in his chest. His powerful hands are rubbing the hair on my head as I am sobbing uncontrollably. I only recall one piece of the conversation. I had asked my dad, "How long has this been going on?" He replied, "Kenny, this has been going on for years." It was then I was hit with the next most intense feeling I have ever experienced. This was the first time I felt it. Shame, utter and complete shame. I literally convulsed as I replied, "Oh my God, Dad, I'm so sorry. Look at how upset I am. I have only seen this once, but you have been dealing with this for years. I feel so selfish!" Physically, emotionally, I became a different person right then and there. That night, everything changed. The trauma took away my sense of self and my inherent power. My trauma changed who I was as a person. I now felt rejected, inadequate, powerless, and worthless.

Trauma Wears Many Different Faces

Some people equate trauma to something big like war, death, extreme acts of violence, physical abuse, sexual abuse, or natural disasters. While those are all examples of trauma, trauma doesn't have to be big like that. It can be any significant negative event or incident that makes us feel bad, scared, ashamed, or hurt. What trauma is to each of us depends on a variety of factors, including age. No matter what kind of childhood we've had, nobody escapes trauma while growing up. If you define trauma as any sense of loss of self, we have all been traumatized as children. Like it or not, events from our childhood shape us. Without being intentional, parents, teachers, and coaches inflict trauma in simple, subtle ways like making sarcastic comments, being dismissive, being late, and not valuing our time. Being controlling, being judgmental, or always having to be right are other ways that adults may inflict trauma on children. It is just like the kind and loving words my dad said to me. His intent was to love me but I felt shame.

We may experience big traumas later in life, like the death of a loved one, divorce, or a tragic accident. But those bigger traumas evoke the same feelings we had in response to the often more subtle original traumas we experienced as children. How we cope with life depends on how we make sense of those traumas. For those of us who haven't been taught how to deal with our trauma, we get stuck living in the worst day ever. The intense feelings of those moments replay themselves throughout our life because, in an effort to heal, we unintentionally and proactively seek them out and re-inflict them upon ourselves.

At any age, we tend to rationalize trauma, to minimize it, suppress it, repress it, and most of all deny it. We have to do all this so we can survive it. Now, as adults, we are completely unaware that we are reliving our trauma daily. Many clients who come into my office believe they have never suffered any trauma. That is how severe the disease of denial is in our culture. I have yet to see a person who is not stuck in this cycle. No one is immune, regardless of personality type or degree of trauma suffered. We stay stuck because no one has taught us about it and we don't know we're affected. It has been my experience that if any part of our personal or professional life is not where we want it to be, it is rooted in the trauma cycle I am about to describe here. Unaddressed trauma survives in a vacuum, fueling our thoughts and behaviors, so we inadvertently re-create the same feelings we had when we first experienced the trauma. We call this the Worst Day Cycle.

10 | YOUR JOURNEY TO SUCCESS

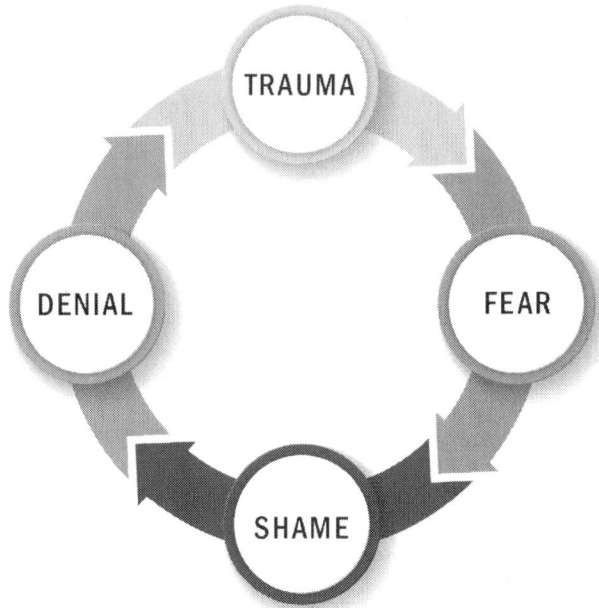

The Worst Day Cycle

Trauma happens *to* us. When it does, our authentic self and power is taken from us.

Fear. Due to the trauma, we experience the fear of rejection, inadequacy, and/or the fear of powerlessness itself.

Shame. Shame is the feeling of having little-to-no worth. We use those negative feelings against ourselves to try to get our power back.

Denial. We deny, suppress, repress, and minimize our trauma to preserve our self-concept. By doing so, we set ourselves up for repeating the cycle again.

The Cycle Keeps Circling

No matter what kind of trauma we experienced as a child, we replay that loop through our choices of friends, hobbies, careers, and relationships. We are attempting to take control of the trauma by victimizing *ourselves* because that gives us our power back. That's what is happening when someone going through a divorce sleeps around and gets drunk every weekend. They feel rejected, inadequate, and/or powerless so as they head out once again they scream, "I'll show them!" They are taking their negative feelings out on themselves. Even though they are unaware, their theory becomes, "I can't get my spouse to love me, so I'll show them. I won't love myself either, but at least I am in control of doing it to myself. I got my power back!"

Stress versus Fear

The American Medical Association (AMA) states that 80 percent of all health problems are stress related. That stress reaction is actually fear. We call it stress because we are allowed to say it happens to us. If I tell you I am stressed, it sends the message, "I am powerful and superhuman in my relationship and career. I'm not a failure." Fear is a different animal in our society. If we tell people we are afraid, it sends the message that we are weak and definitely a failure. To avoid this, we have all dropped into denial and created an empowering word to disguise what is really happening. We then continue our *stress*-related activity, which is self-victimization but at least we are in charge of it. This is another way we try to get our power back, though it inevitably backfires. When we are in denial, we keep self-victimizing ourselves, which keeps us repeating the cycle. When we use the word *stress* instead of *fear*, we are perpetuating the cycle. Society tells us, "it's okay to be stressed because it means I'm doing more than you are." By doing this, we gain sympathy from others for how much we are enduring. In essence, this gives us power. It also gives us permission to revictimize ourselves because we are stealing sympathy from others. If we used the term *fear* instead of *stress*, people would point out how we are doing that to ourselves.

The Research of Science and Emotions

The Centers for Disease Control and Prevention (CDC) estimates that 85 percent of all diseases have an emotional element. That means it is incredibly rare that any illness or disease or injury is caused by anything other than what you feel inside. The Adverse Childhood Experiences Study (ACE Study) backs this up and is considered one of the largest studies ever conducted on the association between childhood maltreatment and health and social problems as an adult. In this long-term study, Kaiser Permanente and the CDC had 17,000 Health Maintenance Organization members undergo a physical exam and share information about their childhood experience of abuse, neglect, and family dysfunction. Participants were recruited between 1995 and 1997. About two-thirds of people reported at least one adverse childhood experience. How many adult childhood experiences (ACEs) were experienced was strongly linked with high-risk health behaviors in adulthood such as smoking, alcohol and drug abuse, promiscuity, and severe obesity. ACEs were also correlated with depression, heart disease, cancer, chronic lung disease, and untimely death. Although this is considered a landmark study in the medical community, few want to talk about it.

Power Retrieval

If you are not dealing with your emotions and the unresolved trauma trapped inside of your body, you are revictimizing yourself. Being sick and hurt is the single greatest way we gain power over others, because what happens when we get sick and hurt? Everyone comes to our rescue. We get our power back. There is a big fear about addressing this truth. In fact, my editors were concerned that by making this controversial statement about how horrible illnesses, diseases, poor relationships, and careers are somehow self-imposed that I might alienate my readers. Although it's not in my best interest to address this, the science backs it up. But I understand why we don't want to hear it—because right now, it is the only way we know how to overcome the trauma we suffered. We refuse to see the reality because we need the power we get from being the victim; it is the only coping skill we know. We can only do what we know. And that is precisely why I chose to write this book. It is time we face our denial and learn another way.

Can New Ideas Really Help?

Offering a new way can be met with skepticism. In the book *Molecules of Emotion*, Candace Pert recounts what happened to Hungarian doctor Ignaz Semmelweis in the 1840s. He practiced in an obstetrics ward in Vienna and noticed,

The impoverished women who were under the care of hospital midwives were not nearly as susceptible to fatal childbed fever as were the wealthier women, who were cared for by doctors, and he figured out that the discrepancy could be due to the fact that the doctors were not washing their hands before examining the women. Since the doctors were on a daily schedule that took them straight from the morgue, where they did research, to the obstetrics ward, where they performed their examinations, their hands were often still covered with the blood and germs of the corpses when they saw their patients—but nobody knew of the existence of germs then… As an experiment, Semmelweis tried washing his hands before seeing patients, with the result that his patients no longer contracted the dreaded fever. But when he implored his colleagues to do the same, they scoffed and laughed, paying no attention to his seemingly outrageous idea. Finally, in 1862 in a desperate attempt to make his point, he cut off one of his fingers and plunged his hand into the open belly of one of the corpses, only to develop a fever and die within a few days. (p. 223, *Molecules of Emotion*)

It can take time to accept new ways of looking at things because of the Worst Day Cycle. It causes us to scoff at anything that is new or that threatens our status quo. Throughout this book, you will be challenged to "wash your hands." Your health and happiness will be determined by your ability to do that.

It's Time to Share the Truth

The trauma and feelings I experienced after discovering my mom in the bathroom sowed the seeds for this book. It has taken me years to research and understand fully what happened and what it all means. I am finally at a place where I can share it with you. I am not perfect. I have blind spots in my Worst Day Cycle. None of this is a race to the finish line; it's a process. I continue to experience shame and denial, but if something bad is happening in my life, I look at myself first before judging or blaming others. As a result, I rediscover the authentic child who was lost that night and get more freedom, joy, and spontaneity in my life.

> **Your Journey to Success Steps**
>
> 1. The first step to success is to accept that you have experienced trauma and that when you don't address it, it keeps you from the life you want.
> 2. What feeling comes up when you consider making a change that you logically know will make your life better? If you feel fear, procrastination, or are overwhelmed, those felings stem from your trauma.
> 3. Choose to become an expert in whatever feelings come up. This expertise will give you an opportunity to bridge the gap to all of the wonderful success processes and books out there. Without that expertise, at some point your original feelings will pop back up and stop you from following all of their incredible advice. Ultimately, underlying that feeling is our fear of success. Make a choice to confront it.

Chapter Two

The Mind-Body Connection

Getting stuck in our worst day ever is our brain's fault. But before I get into that, it's helpful to know a bit about how our brains work.

How the Brain Works

Our brains are small, but mighty. Besides doing the physical things like regulating our body's temperature and heart rate and giving us the ability to see, feel, taste, and touch, the brain controls our emotions and how we think. Up until the late 1970s, we didn't know much about the connection between our brains and body when it came to stress and trauma. Candace Pert, a molecular biologist, helped identify a fundamental element of brain chemistry as a graduate student. While working at Johns Hopkins University of Medicine, she and a team of researchers discovered the opiate receptor, which is the brain's receptor that opiates like morphine fit into and bond with cells in our body. This helped change the way the scientific community looked at how the human body functions. As it turns out, thoughts and feelings release chemicals throughout our bodies that cause actual chemical reactions, proving that the mind-body connection is real.

Think of our brains as a complex computer system that continually sends and receives information. The biggest portion of our brain is the cerebrum, which is divided into two hemispheres and has three sections known as the forebrain, midbrain, and hindbrain. In our midbrain, our thalamus, which is part of the limbic system, takes in information. This is where almost all nerves that connect our brain and body meet. The thalamus diagnoses different sensory information transmitted to the brain through sight, sound, smell, taste, and touch. It acts like a traffic cop directing all incoming information. In addition, the thalamus is the emotional control center of our brain. In any situation, it sends signals to our body when a physical response is required. The thalamus also sends information to the prefrontal cortex, whose job is to assess, plan, and make choices. Most importantly, it sends a signal to the hypothalamus, which monitor's critical internal body functions like temperature, hormones, blood sugar, appetite, sleep, thirst, blood pressure, immune system response, and metabolism. Consider this our state of balance—the "norm" of our brain, body, and mind.

Our Brain's Role in Emotions

For our discussion, we will focus on the brain's role in our emotions. When we experience life, the hypothalamus creates the necessary chemical cocktail that causes us to feel the way we do. For example, when we see our spouse, our hypothalamus secretes a chemical concoction that tells our brain, body, and mind how we feel physically and emotionally. That feeling then generates the thoughts that follow. Simply put, our feelings are just a bunch of chemicals in our brain that get fired repeatedly. We'll want to keep this concept in mind as we learn about ways to get out of the Worst Day Cycle.

Our midbrain is also home to our amygdala, which plays an essential role in the processing of memory, decision-making, and emotional reactions. The right amygdala evokes negative emotions like fear and sadness while the left induces either pleasant or unpleasant emotions. When our thalamus gathers incoming data, it runs everything by the amygdala first. The amygdala acts as an alarm system, as it reviews all new information and determines whether or not it is a threat. Perceived threats trigger our defensive fear response, which we know as fight, flight, or freeze. In the amygdala's view, a threat can be anything from someone holding a gun to our head to a memory of something that has frightened us in the past to even learning something new. Further, the amygdala doesn't differentiate between an immediate threat of danger or perceived danger. Unintentionally, our amygdala can send us a signal that we are experiencing a physical or psychological threat. From there it bounces off of our hippocampus, which is like a secondary smoke alarm to our amygdala. It lets us know what is safe/isn't safe and what is known/unknown so we can react with a ready-made response. The hippocampus helps us draw on those memories stored physically in the cells of our body as well as in our brain. This can be dangerous, as chronic stress (which is actually fear) or any chronic condition is just the accumulation of these chemicals that are stuck unprocessed in our body's cells. That is why we will typically have a physical symptom (illness, disease, or even physical injury) in response to an emotional situation. Our body has now found a place to store the chemicals linked to that emotion. The hypothalamus generates the chemicals that trigger the emotion associated with trauma and shuts down the body to enable us to be in the best state to survive impact. That is great if a bear is coming toward you, but not so great if you are entering a business networking meeting and are frozen in fear.

How Our Brain Works Against Us

Even though we desire to live in our best day, it's hard to get out of the Worst Day Cycle because our brain doesn't know how to behave. If we don't know something or are exposed to something new, we have no emotional chemical marker for our thalamus to categorize the situation as homeostatic (our norm or equilibrium). That's when our amygdala gets triggered. The adrenaline rush of fear shuts down the cognitive thinking and reasoning part of our brain. When we are afraid, we automatically go into denial because our brain seeks homeostasis whenever possible. In other words, it seeks what it knows; it seeks comfort. It doesn't recognize the difference between good and bad. That is why, in general, positive thinking is not as important as learning to *feel* positively, because our thoughts about a situation are derived from what we are feeling. This chemical reaction, the feelings we have been firing for so long, is more powerful than our thoughts. Our brain and body become addicted to the feelings associated with our trauma and our worst day because they have been firing more than any other feeling. We can't remember our best day or live our life to its fullest potential because we don't have that chemical addiction inside our brain and body to do so. It's like telling ourselves, "Don't do that, it is wrong," but somehow we can't stop ourselves from doing it. We end up repeating the behavior that we already know will end badly.

The Role of Trauma in the Brain

Trauma has a way of overwhelming us. When we are threatened, our first response is fight, flight, or freeze. These are physiological or psychological reactions to a traumatic event. As a result, the brain changes to deal with future perceived stressors. Consider victims of domestic abuse who refuse to leave the situation. Cognitively they know it is bad for them, but the mere suggestion of leaving will send them into a fight, flight, or freeze mode because their brains and bodies have become addicted to the abuse. I choose the word "addicted" because they become helpless in the face of their craving for those chemicals—that is, the intense chemical reaction in their brain and body. As a result, their feelings override their thoughts. They want to change, but since their amygdala and hippocampus have no blueprint or intense chemical reaction for what leaving looks like, they stay. Our brain and body like the status quo because their central job is to keep us alive. No matter how horrific our situation might be, their mantra is to stay put; after all, we've survived it before so it must be okay.

The Pesky Role of Neural Pathways in the Brain

As we experience an emotion repeatedly, we create something called a neural pathway—a series of neurons that connect to send signals to other regions of our brain. A great metaphor is sledding in the winter down a hill. With freshly fallen snow, there are no tracks to follow. We can go anywhere we want, as nothing is guiding us down a particular portion of the hill. With each successive trip down that hill, the ruts and grooves become deeper and as a result we can get stuck. No matter how hard we try to steer the sled in a different direction, the ruts are too deep. From this point on, we are destined to take the same path down the hill every single time. Our brain loves this because it knows the path. It's repeatable and familiar. As long as we are alive, we will continue to go down that same path—even if it is a horrific ride. To get unstuck, we need to go back to the top of the hill and forge a new, unfamiliar track. That's our solution. We need to retrain our brains.

This book shares new concepts, so be patient with your brain. You may choose to read the book several times as you get your brain comfortable. That way our amygdala can quiet down, our hypothalamus can fire new chemicals, and our hippocampus can start storing new, more positive feeling memories. This will allow us access to thought and reasoning. If our life isn't where we want it, it's because we have experienced an emotional marker that fires repeatedly and has created a system that is working against us. Our sled has not left that track for years. Until we address that emotional marker, we cannot change. Thoughts alone will have little effect. To create a new neural pathway, we must address the emotion and rework it and the accompanying belief structures. To do that, we need to go toward that original trauma. We need to become an expert in all of it, including the resulting fear, self-victimizing shaming behaviors, and the denial we use to guard it. If we don't do this, we are destined to ride that treacherous track the rest of our life.

The Role of Self-Sabotage

Something we also need to be aware of: the fear and the excitement responses in our brains are exactly the same. Our brain does not know the difference. Ever wonder why people sabotage their progress or even career with senseless choices? It's because as they get excited and are about to reach their potential, if they have not resolved their trauma their gut instinct tells them something is wrong. The excitement creates the same feeling as the trauma. So, they end up victimizing themselves and don't understand why. They ask, "Everything was going so perfectly, why did I do this?" The answer is they haven't worked through their trauma, fear, shame, and denial. This explains why there's such an epidemic of so-called successful and wealthy people who are miserable and self-destructive. They are caught in this cycle as well. Don't be alarmed if this happens to you as you work through this process. It is actually a gift. Your brain is beginning to change and, as it changes, you may experience slips and take a few steps backward. That doesn't mean you've lost everything; just continue to work at it. On the positive side, you will feel this change as you begin to create moments of joy and spontaneity in your life.

Trauma Gut Reaction versus True Gut Reaction

When faced with something new, something often doesn't feel right in our gut. Our "gut reaction" is to turn away from this new option. This urge may actually be our trauma gut reaction seeking what we know. This keeps us repeating our Worst Day Cycle rather than trusting our true gut reaction. I had to learn the difference between the two. The true gut reaction is when we make a decision and we know in our gut it was the right thing to do. There is no negativity or fear of unknowns. We don't question our decision. When it's a trauma gut reaction, we know something doesn't feel right. We make a decision based on that, but we second-guess ourselves. When I first started coaching, in the span of three days I lost every single client. My trauma gut reaction was to do what I have always done—to fix the problem by trying to control it. I started looking for networking opportunities. I made a list of prospects and began composing strategic emails to them. I was operating out of pure fear. My trauma gut was doing what it knows best.

Then I caught myself, paused, and got quiet. After several minutes of just being quiet, I knew with complete certainty (true gut reaction) that what I needed to do immediately was get smarter. I spent the next three weeks lying by the pool reading books getting smarter. That's how I created the Worst Day Cycle. I could have never written this book if it had not been for those three weeks. When we become an expert in our trauma history and know how we self-victimize and drop into denial, we have an opportunity to create a new reality with a new neural pathway in our brain.

Our Body's Response to Our Emotional State

As noted, since we store our memories physically in our body, we are depositing our trauma physically in our body. As Candace Pert points out in

Molecules of Emotion, "Repressed traumas caused by overwhelming emotions can be stored in a body part, thereafter affecting our ability to feel that part or even move it. Certain emotions are associated with pain in different parts of your body." Stem cell biologist Dr. Bruce Lipton discovered that genes and DNA can be manipulated by a person's beliefs. Author Louise Hay believes physical symptoms are just tangible evidence of what is going on in our unconscious mind and buried feelings we have inside. Our body responds to our emotional state. There is ample scientific evidence to back this up. In the book *You Can Heal Your Life*, Hay lists different physical symptoms (illness and/or disease) and why we have them. I have personally found what she shares to be 100 percent accurate with my clients.

I know the impact of emotions on my body all too well. As a kid, I was in and out of hospitals with lower back problems. In my experience, lower back problems are typically caused by finances. I was always afraid of money. I was afraid of having it, not having it, and losing it. In our household, money was always tight even though we appeared to be living the country club lifestyle. When I filed for bankruptcy as an adult, my back flared up, seized, and the whole right side shut down. In both males and females, the right side of our body propels and moves us forward. It is also connected to the masculine part of ourselves or, as I see it, our father. I could never confront my father, so I could never move forward. All but one of my countless injuries, broken bones, and surgeries were on my right side. Then my appendix burst. Stomach problems are caused by fear, especially the fear of something new. When it happened, I had just found out my mother was an alcoholic.

I was born and raised in Denver, but when I would leave in the winters to play hockey and then come back in the summers, I would invariably get sick upon my return. My mere presence in Denver would trigger a feeling memory inside my body. I didn't know that just being in the environment of past trauma can fire off those chemicals. We don't have to even relive the event; we just have to be around it. The neural pathway that formed in my brain at age ten was still alive and well during my second marriage when everything began to fall apart. Once again, I became sick and hurt. I was playing professional golf and I was in so much fear. I started having these deep, dark depressive periods where I would basically become immobile for two to four days. I saw specialists and was on massive amounts of medication trying to control it. The true problem wasn't a brain disorder, as they tried to lead me to believe, and the solution was not all the medications they gave me.

I stopped taking care of myself and, to manipulate my second wife, I was saying *yes* when I should have been saying *no*. As part of trying to get her to like me, I started drinking after over twenty years of sobriety. My wife said she wished she knew me when I was drinking. She said, "It would be fun to know that Kenny." So, I showed her that side. One night we were out and I could feel her disconnection. My exact thought was, "I wonder if she'd like me if I started drinking again?" This is how powerful neural pathways are, even ones that haven't been used in over twenty years. I immediately stood up, walked to the bar, and proceeded to order a double white Russian. Fourteen drinks later we went home.

The abandonment I suffered from my parents created a neural pathway that sends me into massive self-victimization. Because I could not stand up for myself, the fear of asking for what I wanted and needed was absolutely overwhelming. I was emotionally trained to think that I was a bad person if I did not meet my parents' needs. Was that their intent? Of course not. But that's what happened because no one taught them any of this stuff, either. They would have raised me differently if they knew another way.

As you are reading this, you might be thinking this is all voodoo, just crazy eastern medicine drivel. I'm not trying to say that if we are legitimately sick or have a hereditary disease that medicine might not help us. That's not my point at all. What I am saying, and science backs this up, is that if we are only pursuing medication for answers to our health problems, we aren't dealing with the real issue. Our feelings/emotions need to be addressed if we want a complete solution. In her book *Molecules of Emotion*, Pert points out that in the 1940s Wilhelm Reich proposed the link between cancer and the failure to express emotions, especially sexual emotions. In the 1980s, a psychologist from the University of California, San Francisco, showed that cancer patients who kept emotions like anger buried inside had slower recovery rates than those who were more expressive. Both of my parents died from cancer. Pert indicates that denied, repressed, minimized, or ignored emotions related to trauma can chronically constrict blood flow and deprive our brain and other organs of the vital nourishment they need. As a result, we will be less alert and more stuck, which causes us to repeat old patterns of behavior and trigger feelings that are responses to an outdated knowledge base. In essence, this is our Worst Day Cycle.

> **Your Journey to Success Steps**
>
> 1. Create a vision board. Download the worksheet from my website: www.coachkennyweiss.com.
> 2. Spend each day sitting in the best day of your life. Our brain remembers three negative things to each positive. Being positive creates a neural pathway that doesn't keep you stuck in your worst day.
> 3. Become aware of what is triggering your feelings. See Activity 8: Feelization in the Appendix.

Chapter Three

Trauma = Loss of Connection

In his book, *Waking the Tiger: Healing Trauma*, Peter Levine shed new light on the topic of trauma when it was published in 1977. Today, it is considered a classic. He wrote,

> Trauma is a basic rupture—loss of connection—to ourselves, our families, and the world. The loss, although enormous, is difficult to appreciate because it happens gradually. We adjust to these slight changes, sometimes without taking notice of them at all. Contrary to the view of psychiatric medicine—that trauma is basically untreatable and only marginally controllable by drugs—when treated thoroughly, healing can lead not only to symptom reduction, but long-term transformation."

Author and therapist Levine viewed trauma as a fact of life, but not a life sentence. It's not a life sentence unless we don't address it. As we attempt to move away from reliving our worst day and reach for our best day, it's necessary to explore not only our childhood but additional trauma we've endured throughout our life.

We all experience different kinds of traumas—some are big and some are small. For instance, whenever I got in trouble as a child, my dad would call me "Kenneth." Because no one taught him how to parent without shame, more often than not he used shame to discipline me. Just hearing someone say my full name triggers all those old feelings. *That* is trauma. All traumas share a common thread—they make us feel bad, scared, ashamed, or hurt but mostly powerless. It's the *feeling* we had while the trauma happened, not the actual event or incident, that keeps us stuck. Until we reconcile that feeling, we'll continue living in one of our worst days and retraumatize ourselves. For some of us, it may feel like we are in the movie *Groundhog Day* where we keep repeating the same day. The good news is this does not have to be a life sentence; there's a solution and it's all contained in working through and becoming an expert on our Worst Day Cycle. In the following chapters, we'll dissect the Worst Day Cycle and reveal the significance of trauma, fear, shame, and denial and how they are intertwined. Unresolved trauma plays a key role in how we interact with ourselves and the world.

The Worst Day Cycle

TRAUMA → FEAR → SHAME → DENIAL → (TRAUMA)

Trauma happens to us. It takes our authentic self and power from us.

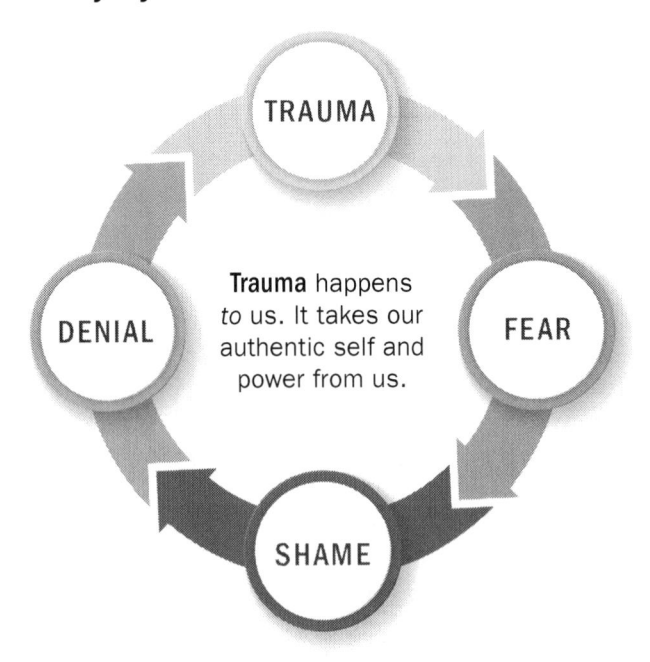

Being trapped in the Worst Day Cycle can be suffocating. It's time to fight to get our authentic self and power back. The first step is to admit the event(s) that initially got us into this cycle. For some of us this can be challenging, as we don't recall what happened; for others it can be painful as we can't forget what happened. Ask yourself the following questions to find out if you are stuck in the Worst Day Cycle:

- Do you find yourself blaming others?
- Are you repeatedly the victim?
- Do you feel guilty when you say *no* to someone?
- Do you feel like things have to be perfect?
- Do you have to be right most of the time?
- Do you offer advice when not asked, especially to your adult children?
- Do you feel guilty pursuing your own life and not being there for your parents?
- Do you have difficulty sitting still? Do you always have to be doing-something?
- Do you have chronic health issues?
- Are you performing below what you are capable of?
- Are you stuck in a job or relationship that isn't working?

If you responded *yes*, it's a clear sign that you have unresolved trauma issues and are stuck in the Worst Day Cycle.

Just What Is Trauma and How Common Is It?

The Substance Abuse and Mental Health Services Administration (SAMHSA) describes individual trauma as resulting from "an event, series of events, or set of circumstances that is experienced by an individual as physically or emotionally harmful or life threatening and that has lasting adverse effects on the individual's functioning and mental, physical, social, emotional or spiritual well-being." In the 2011 publication *Helping Children and Youth Who Have Experienced Traumatic Events*, SAMHSA states:

- 60 percent of adults report experiencing abuse or other difficult family circumstances during childhood.

- 27 percent of children in the United States will witness or experience a traumatic event before they turn age four.
- Four of every ten children in America say they experienced a physical assault during the past year, with one in ten receiving an assault-related injury.
- More than 60 percent of youth aged seventeen and younger have been exposed to crime, violence, and abuse either directly or indirectly.

Both big and small traumas can result in posttraumatic stress disorder (PTSD). Research shows that traumatic experiences affect our behavioral health, too. You don't have to be diagnosed with PTSD to experience fallout from trauma. According to SAMHSA, people who have experienced trauma are fifteen times more likely to attempt suicide, four times more likely to become an alcoholic, four times more likely to inject drugs, three times more likely to experience depression, and two times more likely to have a serious financial problem.

Addressing Trauma Takes Courage

Without a doubt, it takes courage to address our trauma. When we were first traumatized, we were the victim. The trauma happened to us—we weren't responsible for it. In my experience, there are two ways people deal with and deny their trauma.

1. We appear to be successful and strong when we are generally the weakest and hurt. The typical type-A personality is always on the go and use fear, anger, and shame as a propellant. But just like the rocket boosters on the space shuttle, it is a finite power source and it eventually explodes. This go-getter can be tougher to treat because they usually have accumulated "things," such as wealth and status. They use those outward signs of success as proof they must be okay. They keep themselves incredibly busy so they never have to feel. Like Forrest Gump, they are continually running. And because they never stop, they never have to address what they are running from or even fully realize that they

are running. They can always point back to their degrees, title, or portfolios and say, "This doesn't apply to me. Look how successful I am; I haven't experienced trauma; I'm not in denial."
2. The ACE Study shows that almost all injury, disease, and illness is the by-product of unhealed feelings and emotions related to adverse childhood experiences. People have learned to get their power back by becoming sick or a victim. They continually are in situations where it seems everyone and everything is against them. The good news is that because this route of dealing with trauma is so feeling-oriented, they tend to have an easier time facing their denial. That is in part because they primarily suffered abandonment as children, so they are more open and desperate for connection.

In general, most people deal with or deny their trauma in both these ways, at least in part. Neither way is better or worse than the other. Using one approach, we try to overcome our Worst Day Cycle from the one-up or better-than position; using the other method, we try to escape from the one-down or less-than position.

The Many Faces of Trauma

Trauma can be so subtle. There are certain feelings that come up in its aftermath that keep us choosing trauma whether we know it or not. These include rejection, inadequacy, powerlessness, and feelings associated with shame. We choose these feelings by re-creating the trauma or retraumatizing ourselves with it. Until we have a basic understanding of trauma, we cannot succeed. That's why we typically deny what happened. To do so keeps us stuck in the worst day. Clients who see me for business-related topics are completely unaware that their work stumbling blocks are rooted in the Worst Day Cycle. In each episode of the reality television show *The Profit*, the brilliant businessman Marcus Lemonis visits a different business that is in shambles. In very short order, he identifies and then turns around the process problems of running the business. The people are the difficult part. They struggle with following the process or seeing how they are playing a part in the business's failure. They are all caught in their Worst Day Cycle. If you as a businessperson aren't dealing with and focusing on your Worst Day Cycle, you are overlooking the most important part of your potential business success.

How Do We Get Out of the Worst Day Cycle?

Being stuck in the Worst Day Cycle can affect all aspects of our life. The aftermath of our trauma proves to be the most difficult as we continually self-victimize and then deny what is happening. Trauma is the first part of the cycle. Without it, the cycle would not exist. What we need to do is acknowledge the trauma and learn about it instead of avoiding and denying it. We need to turn toward our fear of trauma. To avoid my trauma, I tried to control everyone and everything around me. But this only caused me pain. I am uncomfortable when I turn toward my trauma, give up that control, work through those feelings, and allow my brain time to reorient itself. My counselor would repeatedly say to me, "Kenny, you just need to learn how to *be*." I never understood that until now. Every person's desire to grow is different. How long it will take them to get out of the Worst Day Cycle is up to them and depends on one thing—pain.

As you read this, are you second-guessing whether you really want to undertake that first step of your Worst Day Cycle? You say you want your life to be different but this just seems like too much work. If so, that old feeling has surfaced—the one that keeps you awake at night as you contemplate change, the one that is waiting for you when you wake in the morning. That feeling is your Worst Day Cycle; it is fighting you right now. It doesn't want to leave just yet. If you aren't willing to take that first step on the journey to success, then there is only one way for you to get the life you want—pain and suffering. Whatever it is you are doing to avoid addressing your cycle and your fear of success, do it more. Have more affairs; embezzle more money; take more sleeping pills; experience more illnesses, injuries, and disease; and medicate more with food, pills, alcohol, pot, illicit drugs, porn, or sex. Whatever you are currently using to self-victimize and keep your walls of denial up, accelerate them. Inflict so much pain on yourself that you run out of it and have no other choice but to finally turn toward the one thing we have all avoided. Success. That is right. Our success and inherent greatness come to light when we overcome our Worst Day Cycle. In the following chapter, we'll look at the role our parents played in our trauma.

> **Your Journey to Success Steps**
>
> 1. Make a list of your worst days and your feelings about them. Where do you feel the most powerless in your life right now?
> 2. Challenge yourself to sit still for one hour. Don't close your eyes; just sit there in silence without any outside stimulus. This includes checking your phone for messages or listening to music. Make note of what feelings come up. If you can only last a few minutes, that's okay, but work on extending how long you can sit in silence until you eventually reach an hour.
> 3. If you are feeling overwhelmed, seek the assistance of a helping professional to help you through your Worst Day Cycle.

Chapter Four

How Our Parents Traumatize Us

Until we recognize we have endured trauma, we cannot stop firing the worst day chemicals. To put an end to the Worst Day Cycle, we need to admit that we are less-than-perfect parents and so were our own parents. In my opinion, relationships and parenting are not high-priority topics in our educational institutions. Although these are the two most critical components of our life, most of us have little information about them. As my mom used to say, "We are winging it." Realizing this might make us feel inadequate or even dumb. But think about it—would we feel bad about not knowing how to be a doctor if we never went to medical school? Of course not. That's why none of us should feel bad if we see our own parenting mistakes addressed in this chapter. Some of what you will read in this book may sound radical, but that is only because of our lack of education. Remember how our brain works: if it has no known reference to something, it naturally wants to reject it. It seeks the status quo, but that is what has us stuck in the Worst Day Cycle. Consider any sense of fear, shame, guilt, or denial associated with these new views to be a wonderful window into our own trauma.

A Toxic Cocktail of Codependency and Enmeshment

Parenting today, and for centuries, has been primarily a cocktail of fear, neglect, abandonment, a lack of boundaries, and a healthy dose of unworthiness. This concoction is all about codependency and enmeshment. Melody Beattie first wrote about codependency in *Codependent No More* back in 1986. Author Pia Mellody outlines in her book, *Facing Codependence*, the following five symptoms of codependency:

1. Difficulty experiencing appropriate levels of self-esteem.
2. Difficulty setting functional boundaries.
3. Difficulty owning our own reality.
4. Difficulty acknowledging and meeting our own needs and wants and being interdependent with others.
5. Difficulty experiencing and expressing our reality moderately.

Codependency affects people's ability to have healthy relationships and is often passed down from one generation to another. In his book, *Reclaiming Virtue*, John Bradshaw describes enmeshment as a relationship in which a child (typically of the opposite sex) becomes a surrogate spouse to one of their parents. In enmeshed families, there is a blurring of boundaries that prevents family members from developing a sense of their own self. Let's take the premise that all of us have suffered some level of trauma from either codependency or enmeshment as children. Because trauma happens *to* us, we are defenseless and therefore mostly powerless. According to Pia Mellody, "Children need to be living in a nurturing environment in order to grow up, develop, and thrive. If they don't have an environment that is nurturing, they can't do the business of growing up and that's why I believe there is so much codependency in this culture." These words help us accept that while our parents did their best raising us, many times they provided less-than-nurturing care. Since I firmly believe that all parents have also been traumatized, I think they traumatize their kids without knowing it. This isn't their fault, as they haven't been educated. Ask parents what they want for their children and chances are they will say they want their children to stay out of trouble, get good grades in school, and eventually become successful adults. In essence, we want our children to be better than us. That's a pretty global viewpoint, right? Let's view that statement in the opposite.

While the love most parents have for their kids is genuine, I'm going to argue that a parent's pursuit of a better life for their kids has nothing to do with their child. Hear me out. Because of enmeshment and codependency issues in childhood, our quest for our kids to have a better life is really about us. In the end, our children get to decide who they want to be and what kind of life they choose. We can't control that and, more important, it is not our job to control that. It is our job as parents to provide food, shelter, and clothing along with an environment that allows our kids to express and pursue their own identity, needs, wants, morals, and values. While many would argue that parents should try to pass on their own morals and values to their children, I share this caveat: Most kids rebel in this area; they don't want to follow in their parents' moral footsteps because their parents seem to need it so badly. We are to supply our children with the necessary tools to achieve the life and autonomy we all seek. It is never the child's job to become what we want. In many cases, it is our fear that they won't become *something* that creates dysfunction in our children later in life. We are actually transmitting our unresolved Worst Day Cycle to them and unknowingly asking them to fix it for us by living vicariously through them.

Roadblocks to Growth: Going to the Grand Canyon

A perfect example of what started out as my own less-than-perfect parenting happened several years ago with my sixteen-year-old daughter. I was sitting at my desk when Olivia burst through the door to share that she was getting engaged to her boyfriend. All she saw was future excitement while I saw impending disaster. As parents, we become experts at putting up roadblocks to thwart our children from doing what scares us. I wanted to stop and protect her, to keep her from what I was certain would be the worst decision possible for her. A terrible thing happens when fear meets fear. My daughter was seeking my support, and when I reacted with fear she became fearful, too. The louder I got, the louder she got. I kept putting up roadblocks and she kept barreling through them. I paused mid-sentence as I realized this was going nowhere and what I was doing to us both.

Olivia stared at me for a second and then said, "What? What are you going to say *now*, Dad?"

I stared back at her, thinking it all the way through before I really accepted what I was about to say.

Much more quietly and completely off topic, I began, "Livy, have you ever been to the Grand Canyon?"

With confusion she replied, *"Uh, no!"*

I continued. "Well, what if I told you that I had been—would that stop you from going?"

Unsure and still confused, she replied, "No."

"And what if I told you that I had all of these photos of the Grand Canyon I could show you. Would that stop you?"

She replied, "No."

"And what if I told you how it felt emotionally?" I asked.

"No," she responded.

"Or what if I told you the enormity of it all and how it literally just takes your breath away. Would that make you not want to go?" I asked.

Calmly now, she replied, "No."

I knew I had her, so I leaned in, "Why not?"

With the fear gone from her eyes, she began to bounce. "Uh, because I have never seen it and it looks pretty cool."

I lit up, "That's right!"

I explained, "Olivia, it doesn't matter what my experience is with the Grand Canyon. Until you make the journey and stand there yourself, none of it will ever mean anything or make sense. It is an experience only you can have, just like you wanting to get engaged. I could haul out my old wedding photos, show you the scars, and detail how much it hurt, but it just won't matter, will it? You are still going to want to take your own photos, collect your own scars, and feel the enormity of it for yourself!"

I continued, "So, if you want to get engaged, I think you should do it. All I ask is that you come back and show me all of the pictures, all of the scars, and tell me how you got through all of the pain. Is that a deal?"

You might be asking: Is this good parenting? I believe it is, as I couldn't control her at that age. If she was six or eight years old, I might have been able to. She was almost a legal adult; it simply wasn't going to work and I knew it.

That's why I said what I did to her. When you poke a smoke ring, "poof" goes its shape and it floats away into nothing. The same thing happens when you turn toward fear. My daughter never did follow through on the engagement, but our conversation that day changed how we discuss big ideas. Even today, at some point, she invariably turns to me and says, "Dad, I think I need to go to the Grand Canyon on this one." I always smile and think to myself, one of these days I am actually going to take the time to go and see the real Grand Canyon. Maybe I'll go with her.

In the heat of the battle, I was fortunate enough to recognize that I was trying to control my daughter for my own safety. How do I know that her getting married at sixteen is a problem? Can I be certain of that? After all, my parents were sixteen and eighteen when they got married. People in the back pew of the church were making bets on how long the marriage would last. As it turned out, it lasted a lifetime. Maybe the best thing for Olivia would be to get married at age sixteen. To me, the idea of her getting married was insane, but that is all about me. That is what we do as parents. We make it all about us when it needs to be all about them.

Getting Our Power Back

Because I hadn't learned any of these parenting skills when I was younger, this next story is a classic example of how being codependent and enmeshing with our kids can backfire. Our kids take cues from us. If we are playing the victim and being powerless, so will they. My daughter Olivia was in seventh grade and failing her classes (self-victimization), and she was seeking to get her power back. Her principal called a meeting where eleven adults gathered in a conference room to discuss the situation.

The counselors and teachers were considering all of the systems they wanted to put in place to get her grades up. After about forty-five minutes, they turned to me and asked, "Mr. Weiss, do you have any thoughts?" I responded, "Yes. I find it amazing that no one has asked Olivia how she is going to solve her problem. This is *her* problem and until she cares more about the situation than all of the adults in the room, nothing will change. From what I can see, she has it all figured out. She is sitting over there at the head of the table and she has complete power because she has all of us fixing the problem for her. She is incredibly smart. We have proof of that by the dynamic she has created in this room. I have full confidence that if she ever decides her grades are a problem in her life, she will come up with a better solution than anything we can suggest." These teachers and counselors weren't bad people. They just weren't aware that they were enabling the problem. Today, schools themselves are graded on a student's success and lose funding when students do poorly. The educational system was set up so that educators would have to behave in certain ways to protect their jobs. Do you see how that makes it all about them and not the kids? When people in the room tied their own self-worth to Olivia's success, it became all about them. Olivia was in the catbird seat. She had masterfully brought together eleven adults to fix her problem. That's why she was failing. But it was a paradox, because in this competition she was winning. She had used the self-victimizing piece to gain control and get her power back. I knew in that moment I would never have to fear for Olivia's future.

I tell this story to illustrate a point. If we don't let our kids fail and suffer minor consequences when they are younger, when they are older they will make choices that have life-threatening consequences. When children are young, they have the ability to learn valuable decision-making skills when the consequences are only bruised knees or bad grades. If we don't allow this, we are passing our own Worst Day Cycle down to them.

The Fear of Powerlessness

Sandra's case was no different. She just thought she was afraid of failing. As I explained the Worst Day Cycle, she teared up and shared some background on her grandparents and family history. She was a child of an alcoholic father and her mother was a floozy. They were unable to take care of her, so the grandparents stepped in. Although they adopted her and were spiritual leaders in the church, they never accepted her and told her she'd never be good enough. As a result, she made a conscious choice to spend the rest of her life proving her grandparents wrong.

When I teach my clients about the Worst Day Cycle, I explain how codependency and enmeshment operated in their childhood and how they are carrying on that dynamic in their own parenting. At one of our sessions, Sandra told me a story about her kids' grades. She shared that she and her husband have a rule with their kids. If they have a 3.5 or higher grade point average on their report card, they get rewarded. Anything below that involves no reward. Her boys had brought home their report cards and one son went from a 3.7 to a 3.8; the other son went from a 3.7 to a 3.6. While out to dinner, the kids asked, "What are we going to do to celebrate?" She told her son whose grades went up that they'd do something fun, but she told her other son that because his GPA went down there wasn't going to be a reward. Her son was perplexed, since his grades were above the 3.5 threshold. She was frustrated with the drop in his grades and wanted to know how she could get him to care more. After hearing her story, I asked her:

Did your son meet the 3.5 threshold on grades?
Yes.
When you think about his drop in GPA, what do you feel?
Angry and frustrated.
And what is anger always a veil for?
Fear.
And what are the three elements of fear?
[Silence.]
How about the fear of rejection, inadequacy, and powerlessness? Of those three, which do you fear the most?
Powerlessness.
And when have you felt the most powerless in your life?
[That's when it hit her. She was doing exactly what was done to her while growing up—and she had no idea she was doing it. No matter what she or her mother did, it was never enough for her grandparents.]
Because your grandparents abandoned you both, what have you spent your whole life doing? You've tried to prove them wrong, but no amount of success could ever overcome the self-hatred that they dumped onto you or your mother. Everything you've done in your life was to please them, but you could never do enough. And now, without realizing it, you are passing that behavior down.

That is what parents do. They rob the child's emotional sense of self without knowing it so they can feel better about themselves. Sandra didn't realize it, but she was still trying to please her grandparents through the actions she took regarding her sons' grades.

Creating Our Own Chaos

That same client, Sandra, was leaving corporate America and had just joined a new Realtor team. Most of the agents welcomed her and offered words of encouragement and support. However, one of the Realtors was less than enthusiastic. She said to Sandra, "I was extremely successful in corporate America. You may think you're going to be successful, but wait and see. My first year I made $3,000. So, I hope you saved your money." Sandra felt like she needed to defend her decision to become a Realtor, but then told herself it was this woman's reality, not her own. She responded, "Well, I hope I can make at least that my first year. Please feel free to share any insight or ideas that will help me be successful if you wish." She later realized that this woman was trying to pass her unresolved trauma, fear, shame, and denial onto her.

In that same week, as Sandra moved closer to leaving her corporate job, she felt her family was starting to spin out of control. Her eldest son was missing assignments in school while her younger son was being disrespectful when asked to help out around the house. Even her husband was becoming edgy and short-tempered. At first, she began criticizing everyone, trying to control them and get them back in line, just like her grandparents used to do. On the third day of complete chaos, she switched tactics and began using the tools we had discussed. She took some time to read quietly, do mirror work, and look inside herself to see what was she was feeling. By stepping out of the situation, she was able to observe how she was channeling her anxious energy into her family. She saw that her family was picking up her fears about starting this new career. She was disorganized and chaotic, and so they were as well. Her chaos was due to her past trauma, fear, shame, and denial. It had nothing to do with her family's behavior. As she calmed down and regained control of her emotions, her family became more at peace, too, though she never said a word to them. Sandra is pleased that she's learned a new form of parenting and that when she turns toward that self-victimizing shame and denial, her family naturally follows suit.

When our kids parrot us, it is a reflection of us. Unfortunately, we haven't been taught how to use this self-evaluation process, so our instinct is to focus on them, control them, and usher them back in line. That's because we think if they don't succeed, it reflects poorly on us as parents. The deeper reason is that we feel inadequate because our parents unwittingly did the same thing to us. Because of the Worst Day Cycle, we feel a lack of worth. We try to find that worth by looking outside ourselves since we haven't been taught how to achieve it within ourselves. A natural power dynamic exists with our children. We instinctually look to control our kids or make them better than us because we hold all of the power and they depend on us.

The Battle Over Bruised Knees

I saw that power dynamic at the Denver airport recently. As a family boarded the train to the next concourse, the mother immediately scolded her eight-year-old son about not holding onto the pole on the train. I could tell the young boy wanted to try to keep his balance as the train started and traveled along. He wanted to be spontaneous and experiment; those are both natural instincts of a child and we all learn that way. Because of her own fears, the mother was trying to stifle her child's natural expression and ability to learn for himself. A more appropriate way of dealing with the situation would have been to ask her son, "Before you think about not holding onto the rail, are you okay if you fall and hurt yourself?" This teaches the child to use his own critical thinking and be responsible for his choices and the resulting outcomes. What she unwittingly did was transfer her unresolved fears and trauma onto her child, trying to get her child to make *her* feel safe. That is not the child's job. Yet this is the prevalent dynamic in parenting today. We control our kids not for their safety, but our own.

The Difference Between True Love and Manipulation

Another thing many parents do, and I'm guilty of this myself, is to try to get our children to love and appreciate us for all that we have done for them. That's not love at all, that's a form of manipulation. It is not our child's responsibility to make us feel whole and loved. Parents are often upset that their kids don't appreciate what they do for them. Kids can only appreciate what they have observed. When we as parents are overprotective and overinvolved in our child's life, we're not allowing that child to make choices and decisions. We're stripping our children of their words. Afraid of our own feelings, we dump those feelings onto the child by restricting their movement, thoughts, and beliefs. In adulthood, the child tries to succeed but procrastinates, feeling deep down that they don't deserve anything good—a feeling based on the messages they received as children. By succeeding, they will be going against their parents who needed their child to be scared and dependent upon them. They can't step past that invisible boundary set by the parents. This is very prevalent with adults who were enmeshed with their parents.

That woman on the train in the Denver airport did this to her son and my mom did it to me. To this day, if I get anywhere near a gun, I start to shake and sweat. I have a visceral turning in my stomach and feel a sense of complete dread. All this and I have no trauma surrounding a gun. I've only handled a gun once in my life, when I was about eight years old and had an opportunity to shoot a gun while on a camping trip. But my dad had a shotgun in the house while I was growing up, and my mom was deathly afraid we would get hurt by it. If we got anywhere near that gun, her tremendous fear would take over and she would scream at us. Today, I am reliving her fear—and it's not even mine.

Additionally, because I was so codependent on and enmeshed with my mother, I did not think I had a choice about who I could marry. As a kid, I recall lying in bed and thinking, "I hope she is pretty. I wonder what she will look like and if she will be nice." My role growing up was to be an emotional support for both my parents, so I never learned how to be an emotional support for myself. I never had an opportunity to express my needs and wants. I did not know how to be my own person. Both of the women I married either indirectly (my first wife) or directly (my second wife) asked me to marry them.

What We Say and Mean

What we say and mean are two different things. Often, we make statements, like those you'll see in the following email exchange, that we think are loving. But they are instead quite abusive because we simply have never been taught about healthy relationships and parenting. We basically do what was done to us. We take on the skill set of those who raised us. That is why trauma, illness, and disease are generational. We just pass the emotions on down the family tree. What we have is an epidemic of codependency and the Worst Day Cycle of trauma, fear, shame, and denial.

My client, Trish, age twenty-three, told me in our first six sessions that she had a great relationship with her parents and there were no issues at all. Most adults, when asked, will say their childhood was basically idealistic. They say that because they aren't aware of codependency, enmeshment, or the shame dynamics that are so prevalent in parenting. It wasn't until our seventh session that she began sharing more about her relationship with her parents. She originally came to see me because she had lied on her résumé about having a college degree and was terrified her employer would find out. To complete her degree, she needs to take one simple elective basket weaving–type course, but she won't do it. After reading this exchange of emails between her and her parents, you'll see why. Her trauma cycle is in full bloom. As you read this, note that I'll be sharing my viewpoint between paragraphs to reveal what the sender is actually saying. More often than not, it's the opposite of the words they are choosing to type.

Father: I am having a problem with your attitude. For the past six years, your mother and I have done nothing but support you during high school and college. Everything was paid for. Yet you still find fault with us. I am mean and your mother has whatever issues with you. You live here at little or no cost and yet you're angry at us. Not sure what your bitch is at this point. Since you're unable to be civil to me or your mother, you have six months to move out. Be out by August 30. You are on your own. Do whatever you have to do. You have never had respect for the help your mother and I have given you. Your current attitude has left me no choice. You have a life that we have taught you and the financial benefits. Once you move, and I hope it is soon,

I can either ship your animals to you or charge you ten dollars per day until you find arrangements. Your mother and I have been your biggest supporters since you were born. Since you don't understand that, it is time to cut ties. It is time you move out and live your life. Since you know best and you want to be your own woman, move on and make your life as you see fit. We are always here when you need help but you want to be yourself, so do it. Move on.

Her father is angry because Trish (after working on her boundaries and trying to discover who and what she wants to be) isn't feeding his needs anymore. He is now taking his responsibility (providing food, shelter, and guidance to a child) and turning it into a manipulative bargaining chip. In effect, he is saying, "You won't give me what I want, you won't meet my emotional needs of needing to be placed on a pedestal and worshipped, so I am going to cut you loose. He even chastises her for wanting to be "her own woman." But, he ends it with another manipulative carrot: "We are always here when you need help . . ." but that help has conditions. You need to meet our emotional needs, not be your own person, or our support goes away. This is called a "double bind."

Daughter: I will be out of the house by August 30. I apologize it's not sooner but I need a bit of time to find other arrangements. I will go ahead and set up an automatic payment of $600 a month for my animals' accommodations.

She responds with incredible boundaries to start. She didn't pick up the manipulative bombs that her father was trying to seduce her into. He needed her attention so he exercised what is called negative control to try to get it. She took the tools I was sharing with her and used them perfectly.

Mom now joins the email conversation when the daughter doesn't bite.

Mother: Trish, since you refuse to speak to me, here are my thoughts. Your father is correct that you need to be gracious to us with all we have done for you. College, a house, countless parking tickets, etc. Please be nice. You are grouchy a lot of the time. You're not nice about our choices for upgrading the house. Just suck it up and be helpful and pleasant. You have been given a good life. You have a good brain, a great education, a pretty face, people who love you, and a good job. Be grateful and throw a thank-you our way once in a while. That's all we ask. Your life may not be perfect, but it's pretty damn good.

Mom continues by berating the husband before going back to her daughter.

Mother: Alan, you just shoot off these bombastic, nasty emails. There is no need for them. They are NOT helpful. Trish, I am sorry that you feel that I do not think that you are "good enough." I never meant that; I'm sorry if I come across that way. You do frustrate me with your sitting and complaining. Get up and DO something about it if you are unhappy. Only YOU can make yourself happy, no one else. You are everything to us, but we cannot create your inner peace. Pray, meditate, exercise, practice mindfulness, do some crafts, or whatever. Just be grateful for your good life. You have been blessed. God has been good to you. Move out if you like. It's foolish from a financial perspective. If you stay, enjoy the house. We have made it safe. Just be happy and pleasant to us when we visit once in a while.

Again, look at how Trish's mom also wants to make her daughter feel loved for doing her job, being a parent. All of the money, schooling, house, parking tickets are bargaining chips. The parents did these things in an attempt to get their child to love them. They weren't freely given. They are conditional with the primary condition being that Trish owes them love and emotional peace. Mom even includes her issues with her husband in the email. Those are not discussions that a child needs to be privy to at all. It is a backhanded way of telling her daughter, look at what I have to put up with from your father. Even he won't do what I want so I am co-opting you to get involved so that you can feel sorry for me. Since the parents can't meet their own emotional needs with each other, they have now dropped them onto their daughter. This is the hallmark of codependency and enmeshment. These attacks prove to be too much for Trish. She picks up the manipulations and joins the fight.

Daughter: I respectfully asked you to leave me alone about six times, but that couldn't happen because we all have boundary issues. So, here we are, resorting to emailing, then screaming, then emailing again, like the passive-aggressive, extremely dysfunctional "family" that we are. Dad, you're an alcoholic. Get some help. You're embarrassing and, more importantly, killing yourself. Once you learn how to be a nice person again, I would really love for you to meet my future kids. But at this rate, that ain't going to happen. Mom, you're a manipulative person who masks it with "honesty" when, in reality, you hate yourself and you take it out on your daughter. One conversation tonight wasn't going to change anything. I've tried talking to you for the past five years about all of this, to no avail. Did it ever dawn on you that maybe my being a shit is not actually about the house, my job, or the dogs? That maybe all I need is a little bit of support and open ears from my own mother? I don't need your "honesty" and I never have. I need my mother to listen to me and support me. I am "moving on," "cutting ties" per your request. I couldn't care less about the financial aspect. I'll stay in a job that makes me miserable and save zero money if it puts this bullshit to an end. I'm tired of this "fantastic" life you guys have afforded me being held over my head. I'm sure you guys are sick of your "ungrateful" piece-of-shit daughter taking advantage of it. Like I said before, I'll be out by August 30 and paying the monthly pet convenience fee. Thank you both for everything you've done for me.

Trish has been screaming to be heard. Because her parents were enmeshed and raised in codependent homes, they just don't have the tools to listen. It's not that they are bad parents. They love and adore their daughter; however, they just haven't been shown how to do it in a truly authentic way. This is crazy-making for Trish. She gets that her parents love her. She appreciates all they have done for her, but she is confused. When her parents "love her," it costs her. This is the trauma cycle in full bloom and it's why we turn to shame (self-victimizing) behaviors.

Dad comes back sober the next day with this reply:

Father: Hello Trish. I apologize for some of the things I said yesterday, but let's talk about things. You were a difficult child and you are continuing that difficulty throughout adulthood. I couldn't bribe you to eat shrimp in a restaurant for a Barbie car when you were six, so why should I expect any less of you now? Call it as you see it. Your email tells me you really don't like your mother and me as parents. My intention as a parent was to make you strong, guide you to your interests, and help you achieve what you wanted. I remember you and I eating pizza before a San Francisco Giants game discussing plans for your future a couple days before you went to Stanford. I made good on my promise to you. You were troubled during your Stanford years. Dad took care of whatever you needed. There were a few of Dad's emails giving you shit but we got through them and you graduated. I've been your biggest supporter throughout your life. You have never acknowledged that you have been a financial strain on me. I accepted your tuition as a given. I had no problem giving you the gift of no student loans. What I didn't like was your credit card bills, with the bar tabs and overdue parking tickets. Every month I complained and I still paid. Go ahead and take me to court for being a bad parent, being mean, and being a drinker. I've never done anything to you other than ask you to be civil and be my daughter. You do not need to move out of the house. If you find it horrific with the changes then, Godspeed, move out of the house. My goal was to make you comfortable in your life. This is my last email to you. All I want to do is make you happy. Do what you have to do. Your dogs are not leaving my house. They're happy here and I will take you to court. There'll be no more charges going forward for the dogs. You want to cut ties with me on your various accounts? Call the companies, figure it out, and make it happen. Sorry I disappointed you as a father; have a good life and be good.

Her father readily admits everything he ever did was to manipulate her to get her to love him and that it backfired. He tried to bribe her as a child to get what he wanted from her. He sent her to school and continued to pay her bills so he could control her. He does not know how to take care of his own needs, say no, and so he uses his parental responsibilities as a billy club to imprison his daughter. This is enmeshment and you can see how crazy-making this would be for a child. He says he was happy to do it yet she is a "strain" and "troubled child." He then doubles down and threatens to keep the dogs. His abandonment fears have kicked in so he sets up a way to keep her attached by creating an issue to fight over. He then plays the victim by calling himself a bad father. He does this to get her to feel bad and come running back. The full trauma cycle is played out in this one email. Now Trish has exploded. The double-bind nature of the codependency is too much for her to take. This is exactly what her dad wants. He has her engaged and chasing him. He feels powerful and loved through her anger at him.

Daughter: What the fuck was the point of this email? To just make me feel like shit and remind me how horrible of a daughter I've been and how much debt I have caused? Remind me how difficult of a human being I am?

Job well done. Thank you for all that you've done for me. Thank you. I appreciate it. I really do. Now get some help for your drinking problem. Seriously!

Now Trish's mom jumps in.

Mother: Your father was apologizing. Now cut it out. I wanted to go to Tucson with my daughter this weekend. And I'm tired of my massive diarrhea from being so upset. I won't have to poo for another month because of today. We both love you tons.

This is the most prevalent way enmeshment is exercised. Mom is now "sick" BECAUSE of her daughter. She has now just dumped her own inability to handle her fear—that is what often causes diarrhea—onto her daughter and made her responsible for her health. Parents do this all of the time. Being sick, hurt, and addicted is the greatest and most powerful way we all get our power back and control others. They are not only telling Trish how much it has "cost" them to be parents, but now their health and well-being is her responsibility too. She includes her genuine desire to spend time with her daughter but the message is mixed. The request is all about Mom's needs for attachment and fears of being abandoned. Neither of the parents are listening to Trish. It is all about them.

Daughter: That was not an apology. That was an eight-paragraph timeline of all the things I've ever done wrong. He can shove that apology right up his ass. You're uninvited to Tucson. And I could not care less about your bowels.

Mom replies immediately.

Mother: That was an apology. His kind. And I thought you cared about my health. Thanks. Love you.

Are you starting to see the pattern? Mom makes it all about her and attempts once again to get Trish to parent her and make her feel better. She completely ignores what Trish is saying because she needs Trish to feed her emotionally and nurse her back to health. It is not her daughter's job, but Mom doesn't know how to do it because no one taught her how.

Daughter: Well, his "apology" is not accepted. Not even close. I was having a great night until you people emailed me. Now leave me alone and stop talking to me.

Mom once again completely ignores her daughter's needs and wants and it only takes three minutes to reply. This poor girl's life is all about feeding her mom and dad emotionally. The parents are so stuck in their own trauma they have no ability to nurture their daughter appropriately.

Mom replies:

Mother: Sorry. You're stuck with us. Just like we are stuck with you. All of our warts included. Yours too. Be safe. Love you lots.

Once again, the mom refuses to listen to her child's needs and be the parent. Her daughter asks for no more communication but Mom needs to have the last word. Mom needs to keep the fight going, Mom needs attention, Mom needs to dump her fear and shame onto her daughter so she can carry it for her. She once again manipulates her daughter and continues the crazy-making dynamic by constantly throwing in how much she is loved. Trish can't accept any of the wonderful ways in which they did provide for her because they were never freely given. They were always an attempt to get the child to make THEM feel loved. I liken enmeshment to the movie, Predator. The premise is that this alien creature can cloak himself and disappear when needed. He survives by literally devouring humans and leaving nothing but the skeleton remaining. That is what these parents did. They are cloaked as parents but, in reality, they are children stuck in their trauma cycle. They show up and suck the life out of their daughter to feed their own unmet emotional needs.

This type of parenting leads to the Worse Day Cycle and the generational issues that get passed down. It's why

- we can't ask for or even know what our own needs and wants are.
- we can't say *no*.
- we feel mean or guilty if we don't do things for other people.
- we procrastinate.
- we get that uncomfortable feeling when we considering changing or succeeding.
- we can't sit still.
- we avoid boredom.

Trish doesn't recognize all that her parents have done for her because they have tried to buy her affection and love to feed their own unmet needs. They use this against her instead of setting normal healthy consequences. They pay her parking tickets and keep bailing her out, sending the message that it's okay to get more. In general, kids act out or break rules because they're screaming for boundaries, which give them a sense of safety. Giving them whatever they want creates fear. But because the parents have never been taught how to address their own trauma cycle, they are now transferring it onto their children.

Trish is a prisoner of codependence and enmeshment. It's the reason she can't finish her college degree and begin succeeding in her own life. She is stuck in the shame and denial aspects of her worst day. To avoid losing her only attachment to her parents, she repeatedly confirms their beliefs that she is unworthy. Childhood trauma, like the type of trauma Trish went through, dramatically affects health across a lifetime. For most of us, this type of parenting is what causes our health issues and our Worst Day Cycle. This so-called normal parenting is dysfunctional and abusive. In her TEDX talk, pediatrician Nadine Burke Harris discusses the ACE Study and how childhood trauma affects our brains. She stresses the importance of prevention and treatment of trauma early on so we no longer need to keep reliving our worst day.

Since my parents didn't know how not to be codependent, they passed this trait onto us kids. My dad slamming his hand on the table because we chewed with our mouths open was all about him. He felt angry and scared. *He* did not want his kids to grow up without manners because of how that would reflect on him. While teaching correct manners is good parenting, being so emotionally charged by it is not. His fears were then dumped straight onto us. We were expected to make him feel okay through our obedience. As author Pia Mellody points out in *Facing Codependence*, most parenting is basically a reverse umbilical cord. Instead of the parents feeding their children love and safety, that flows in the opposite direction. To stop the generational passing down of our Worst Day Cycle to our kids, we need to become more informed and educated as parents instead of "winging it."

Your Journey to Success Steps

1. Read *Parenting with Love and Logic* and *Facing Codependence* (See the Appendix for more information.).
2. Journal about how your parents taught you to take care of their emotional needs.
3. Look at your own parenting to see why certain things are so important to you. Ask yourself these questions:
   - Are the things I view as important about my child's wants and needs or my own?
   - Do I feel anxious and fearful about my children?
   - Do I rescue them or clean up their messes when they have difficulties?
   - Do I fear what others will think if my child does or doesn't do X? (That is a red flag that you are passing on the Worst Day Cycle.)
   - Which of your parents' fears are you passing down to your children, and how are those fears showing up in your Worst Day Cycle?
4. Watch the TEDX Talk featuring pediatrician Nadine Burke Harris to see the impact of childhood trauma.

Chapter Five

White Hot Fear

Fear is always about one of three things: rejection, inadequacy, and/or powerlessness. These three potential states or feelings stem from the trauma we all have experienced. Fear is an unpleasant emotion caused by the belief that someone or something is dangerous and could cause us pain or become a threat. Interestingly, people generally also become afraid when things go well and they are succeeding. It's the opposite of what you might think. We become so accustomed to living in our Worst Day Cycle that when change comes, it scares us. For me, I crave smoking when things begin going well for me. While smoking elevates my heart rate and excitement initially, over time it works against me. It loses its allure and begins making me depressed and angry. For some people, sugar, sex, food, gambling, alcohol, or drugs work the same way. I find it fascinating how we celebrate our achievements. After closing a big business deal or winning in a sport, we often do something that unintentionally gets us out of the feeling state of excitement and achievement. We drink, do drugs, or take part in any number of things that victimize us. People in recovery often have relapses because they are succeeding, not failing. Success is something we just aren't familiar with because of the Worst Day Cycle. It takes time for our brain to orient to our best day.

The Worst Day Cycle

TRAUMA → **FEAR** → **SHAME** → **DENIAL** → (cycle)

FEAR. Due to the trauma, we experience the fear of rejection, inadequacy, and/or the fear of powerlessness itself.

Fear and Parenting

Since trauma happens to us as children, especially if it comes from our parents, we feel fear at the time it happens and later when we are stuck in the cycle. In childhood, our survival depends on our parents, so no matter what they say or do our internal conscious and subconscious thought is, "I must accept this, even if it's wrong." Whatever the parent is struggling with is directly or indirectly handed down to the child. Consequently, we feel rejected, as from our viewpoint our parents are rejecting us. We get the "I'm not good enough" feeling because we don't know why we aren't the priority. That's when we feel powerless—both about doing anything to alter the situation or event that is causing trauma for us and about all of our feelings related to it. I remember the feeling of fear all too well from my childhood. I felt rejected when I found my mom passed out on the toilet. She chose alcohol over me. No matter what I tried, I could not get her to stop drinking. I felt inadequate. It didn't matter if I threw the booze against the wall, poured it down the drain, or gave her hugs (which she asked me to do to help her not drink). I was powerless to do anything about the situation. She wouldn't stop. Part of the way I victimized myself was sacrificing my own needs and wants for my parents. Let's take a closer look at the three main types/sources of fear.

Fear of Rejection, Inadequacy, and Powerless

The fear of rejection is one of our deepest fears. Being rejected sabotages our desire to belong. When we are rejected, we feel unlovable, alone, and worthless. Rejection can happen in all areas of our life and can be painful. If you've ever applied for a job that you were counting on and were rejected, you know that feeling all too well. As children, we adjust our behavior so our parents won't reject us. That is why rejection is so difficult: because of the codependent and enmeshed environments we were all raised in, we are overreliant on others. We don't want to feel the hurt that comes with rejection, so our natural tendency is to avoid it.

The fear of inadequacy is about not being capable or good enough. When we start a new job, feelings of inadequacy are strong—we don't know if we possess the skills or knowledge to get the job done. For example, if we landed a job in the construction industry, we might feel completely inadequate if we knew nothing about construction. We might ask, "How can I build a home if I don't know how to pick up a hammer?" Not having the knowledge or tools to solve a problem can trigger feelings of inadequacy quickly. For me, I felt inadequate about not being able to stop my mom's drinking. Just fill in the blank: I'm *not* _____. I'm not smart enough, not pretty enough, not strong enough, and so on. All those feelings lead to the fear of powerlessness stemming from our original trauma.

The fear of powerlessness is about anything where you don't have control. Think of powerlessness as an *I can't* statement. For example, "I can't get someone to hear me, understand me, like me, love me, give me a raise, or recognize what I do." Powerlessness is probably the most devastating of all the fear reactions. Since we are an organism looking to survive, feeling powerless leaves us in a constant state of hyperarousal. Our sense of safety is gone; we are on high alert trying to gain control of every situation because of the powerlessness we feel to keep ourselves safe. We have not been taught the difference between real and imagined or emotional fears, so any new situation has us petrified. Our body becomes attuned to this so our new normal becomes an adrenaline-packed fear state.

Consequence of Fear

Our brains and bodies don't know the difference between fear and excitement. Feelings of excitement trigger the exact same physiological response in us as our original trauma. That is why we don't "feel" good when we are excited. We create a self-destructive behavior to try and get control of that feeling. We go back to what we know. These feelings shut us down and rob us of the chance to even entertain new thoughts and concepts that could improve our life. That is why, whenever you hear something you are unfamiliar with, you naturally withdraw from it. Both of these processes play a key role in keeping us reliving our Worst Day Cycle.

I see fear in people's expressions and their body language daily. Some people can't sit still and their leg is always bouncing, their fingers are tapping, and they are reaching for their phone as a distraction. They can't keep moving, yet they can't sit still. It's as if they are trying to run out of their skin. If this is your experience, I encourage you to go to the gym and try to keep your eyes fixed in front of you while you do a set of any exercise on a machine. Or go on a simple walk outside or in the mall. If your eyes are continually bouncing and it feels uncomfortable to lock into one item in the horizon, that is fear. For me, boredom would send me into a complete rage. When I discovered my Worst Day Cycle, I realized why boredom was so difficult for me. As a child, if it was quiet that usually meant my mom was drunk. Today, I find boredom wonderful and peaceful. I love the quiet.

Anger Is Fear

Fear of rejection, inadequacy, and powerlessness are the main three triggers for anger. Anger is all about power. Anger in any form at any time is always a veil for fear. Think about it. Why did you yell at the person who cut you off?

Or why did you yell at your child, spouse, friend, or co-worker? Select any situation where you became angry. Think it through and then ask yourself, "Where in this situation did I fear the possibility of being rejected, of being inadequate, or of being powerless?"

Although we get big and sometimes loud when we get angry, what we are feeling is actually the opposite. When someone is angry with you, it's like witnessing a young child screaming, "Please, please don't find out how inadequate and powerless I feel right now and, by God, don't you dare reject me!" For most of us, when we become angry, we emotionally drop back to the age of when our trauma happened. When someone gets angry at me, I envision that young child screaming for help. Would I yell back at a four-year-old or would I want to comfort that child? I now have tremendous empathy for someone who is angry at me. I recognize that the words they are yelling actually reveal how they feel about themselves. None of it is about me. For me to begin yelling back would be like two kids fighting over Tonka trucks. This isn't to say anger is a bad emotion. It is a wonderful release and can do many positive things for us. But for the majority, it is toxic because it is derived from something we have not yet addressed and therefore it is working against us and not for us. A perfect example of this is the Nike "Just do it" philosophy. This message is counterproductive and sets us up to relive our Worst Day Cycle. The whole idea of this marketing slogan is just to get out there and do it and be a grinder. But there's a falseness behind that approach. Does that mean if you aren't doing it, you are somehow bad? This type of message inherently creates a fear of rejection or inadequacy. It sends us into a shame spiral, making us wonder if we did it yesterday, then why can't we do it today? We begin to think something is wrong with us. I spent years *just doing it* and it nearly killed me. For me, that way of living got me addicted to sex, alcohol, tobacco, sugar, spending, and love. I ended up going through two horrific divorces, custody battles, and bankruptcy. I played two professional sports that I never wanted to play just so I wouldn't have to think or feel. The *just do it* philosophy had me at the brink of suicide.

The Fear of New Ideas

Author Joe Dispenza, in his book *Evolve Your Brain*, points out that by our mid-thirties we have experienced and categorized every single emotion possible life can offer. By this time in our life, we are living on autopilot. Our neural pathways are now set and so we become robotic in our thinking. We just relive feelings, thoughts, and choices over and over because, as you recall, our brain never wants to work that hard. It is constantly trying to conserve energy. That is why our brain has categorized our life experiences and our reactions to them.

During a speech on the Worst Day Cycle, I was sharing how fear shows up as anger. I had just discussed what happens when we experience tremendous fear and how we resort to anger to defend our personhood. That's when a man sitting about three rows from the back stood up, loudly said, "This is a bunch of bullshit!" and then proceeded to walk out the door. The man, who appeared to be in his late sixties, was so entrenched in his Worst Day Cycle and being angry that he just could not hear any new information. It was a complete threat to his system.

I find it absolutely fascinating that we have teachers and take tests to become competent in almost every area of our life. But, when it comes to the most important areas—relationships, parenting, and emotions—most of us operate on instinct alone. We receive absolutely no training by experts; the people who do teach us, our caregivers, are amateurs themselves. The monumental ACE Study shows that adverse parenting affects most of us throughout our life. Dr. Robert Block, president of the American Academy of Pediatrics, says, "Adverse childhood experiences are the single greatest unaddressed public health threat facing our nation today." We learn about relationships, parenting, and emotions from people who never went through any sort of training or teaching, either, and we consider that to be good enough. Here's a case in point. Typically, when I see my hairstylist, Julia, she talks about how she can't find a guy who will treat her right. During our last conversation, she told me her latest boyfriend is a jerk. We now know each other pretty well so I finally said, "Julia, would you let me cut your hair?" She stepped back and looked at me like I was completely insane and said, "No." I pressed her and asked,

"Why not?" She responded, "Do you know how to cut hair?" I said, "Nope, I've never done it and have absolutely no training in doing it, but I've watched people cut my hair for years, so I think I have a pretty good idea how to do it."

Now she was really confused. She tilted her head sideways, placed her hands on her hips, and said, "You're crazy. I'm not letting you anywhere near my hair." I said, "You know, Julia, I find it fascinating that we all go into relationships even though none of us have been trained in how to have one. We all think we are experts simply because we've watched other relationships. What we are basically doing is saying, 'Hey, I know you don't know the first thing about relationships and neither do I, but here's my heart—don't screw it up.' Oh, and if this doesn't work out, it's because you were the problem, not me." I then said, "Isn't it amazing that I would have to have a license to cut your hair, considering that no matter what I do to it, it will grow back perfectly?" That we receive not a single bit of training when it comes to matters of the heart, family, and relationships is really criminal, and our reluctance to look at that is pure denial. We deny it is something we should address.

I could see this realization was hard for Julia. She felt inadequate and it made me sad. If we don't know something, our brain automatically shuts down and triggers feelings of powerlessness from our Worst Day Cycle. Instead of being excited by learning something new, we withdraw. To counteract that fear response, we need to work at being open to not having answers to everything and getting help from others. Use these questions to help you start that process now:

- When you went to school, did you learn on your own or was someone there to guide you?
- When you played a sport, did you do it alone or was there someone there coaching you?
- What about your career? Did someone train you in your position? Did you seek out people who have achieved what you want and ask them for advice and direction?

Typically, when we want to become better at something or gain new knowledge, we find an expert on the topic and learn from that person. We need to do the same when it comes to parenting, relationships, and emotions. By not gathering more knowledge, we are choosing to stay in our Worst Day Cycle.

Fear and Our Health

The problem with stuffing fear is that it doesn't disappear. When we stuff all that powerlessness, it reappears in other ways. For example, most health conditions are purely fear based. Divorce, a lackluster career, and addictions are other results of stuffing fear. Remember, most fears are implanted in us. Our trauma happens to us, and we can conclude that our caregivers pass their fears onto us. There were generations before us whose whole existence was filled with trauma and fear, and we inherit all of that. Alcohol, illegal drug, and prescription-related addiction and deaths are some of the things we do to ourselves. Addiction of any kind is born out of overwhelming emotions that can't be experienced, so users seek an alternative reality to medicate those feelings away. I grew up being told that addiction is hereditary. I remember the helpless and powerless feeling that gave me. I felt like I had no choice. It was just going to happen to me and I couldn't do anything about it. Prior to the ACE Study, which proved adverse childhood experiences had real health implications, many in the medical community refused to allow for emotions in their conclusions. Sadly, today that is often still true. Somehow, it's easier to think this helpless nature has been implanted, and to get the message that we are doomed to X condition unless we take some pill for it. Medicine is not the answer. It may be necessary as a starting point, but the complete answer lies in addressing the feelings that have created the problem.

One of my clients hired me to evaluate her son's golf swing. I watched him take two swings. I asked, "Is your lower back hurting on the right side? How about your left shoulder?" He replied *yes* to both questions. I asked, "Is your biggest miss usually to the right?" Again, he replied *yes*. That's when I heard two words out of his mom's mouth, "Oh Jesus." I could feel what was happening inside him emotionally, but I wanted to wait. He finished warming up and we went to play a few holes without his mother. When we got to the second hole, I told him to describe to me the shot he wanted to hit. He explained he was trying to hit it about 10 feet left of the hole. I told him,

"I want you to feel that in your body with your practice swings." He then stepped up and hit the shot. I knew right away what was happening and I didn't sugarcoat my question. As soon as he hit the ball, I asked, "What did you say at the top of your swing?" He looked at me confused, so I asked again. He was caught off guard, so I asked, "Did you say, 'Don't hit it right'?" "How did you know?" he replied. I explained, "Here's what is happening. Your lower back hurts because you are carrying the financial weight. You are stressed out about all the money your parents are paying for your golf. Your dad is the one carrying that. That is why the pain is on your right side. You are worrying about the financial stress you are putting on him. Your left shoulder is hurting because of your mother and trying to please her. As you get to impact, you are physically pulling out of the shot because of the fear involved, the trauma involved in your pursuing golf, and the resulting pressure you feel from your parents to succeed at it. Even with all of that, the ball finished right where you had felt you wanted it to go."

I continued, "You just learned that it doesn't matter what you actually do; if you picture and feel the shot you want the way I walked you through it, you will get the ball where you want it to go. Your body will react to that feeling, even if you have these emotional burdens weighing you down. What you have to decide is if you want to stop carrying this weight for your parents. If you don't want to do that, you will keep thinking about it for every shot and, in many cases, those feelings will win out. That's why your scores have been so inconsistent. If you decide you want to let go of that, just swing and you will hit it wherever you want." We played a couple of holes and he began crying. He shared with me that he didn't want to play golf. I had this same experience when I was married to my second wife and became a professional golfer. There are very few athletes who are playing that love their sport. Instead, they are running from or trying to exercise their Worst Day Cycle. Keep in mind that none of these feelings are bad. There is no such thing as a bad feeling. All feelings are good when expressed appropriately. It's healthy to express our feelings, but society tells us not to share what we feel. This leads to poor self-esteem and sadness. We need to feel our feelings without destroying ourselves for having them. By doing so, we quiet the fear.

Do We Fear Failure or Success?

Are we afraid to fail or is it actually the opposite? People often say they are afraid to fail. I believe it's really success that we're fearful of. First, I have never met a person who is afraid to fail. Do you know why? If any part of our life isn't where we want it to be, we are already failing each and every day. We've become so comfortable with it that we don't even realize we are failing. When we wake up each morning and know what we need to do to succeed and we don't follow through, we have accepted failure; we aren't afraid of it. The problem is feeling based, not thought based. Our feelings trump our thoughts. Thoughts won't change our behavior because they are by-products of what we feel. This tells me that what we really fear is success, because we have no emotional marker to draw from. Our brains and bodies don't know how to fire the necessary chemical cocktail that brings about success.

I recently met with someone who was working with a business/executive coach. He hired this professional to clean up some processes in his company, and he was already seeing the benefit. Like the success books out there, this coach's information was stellar, but my friend was describing how he just couldn't do some of the things the coach wanted him to do. I asked why. He replied, "I don't know, I just don't feel like doing them." Such a simple answer and so profound. This is the same answer most of us give for why we aren't achieving our professional goals, yet we don't see how powerful and information packed that response is. First, "I don't know" tells me that when this man was a child, he wasn't allowed to have his own needs and wants, and he still carries trauma from this. The most impactful part of his statement was, "I just don't feel like doing them." This is the missing piece in the typical executive coaching success model. Everyone who is not reaching their personal or professional success has the same response and struggle. A feeling from their Worst Day Cycle comes up that is so strong, it overrides logic and keeps them from performing the tasks that they know will lead to the success they seek.

There is no amount of positive thinking—the hallmark of most success books and executive coaching—that will overcome this because the answer is *feeling* driven, not *thought* driven. The success books don't touch this. I pointed this out to him and, like so many others, he said, "Yeah, I don't want to go there." When we master the feelings created in our Worst Day Cycle, we can finally take action steps necessary to achieve our goals. Until we do that, no success model will ever completely work. It is all contingent on addressing the Worst Day Cycle.

Again, that is precisely why I have learned that no one ever has been afraid to fail. The man I met with cognitively knew what he needed to address, but he wasn't willing to do it. That feeling—remember he said, "I don't feel like it"—is more overpowering. That feeling is our addiction to failure and the Worst Day Cycle. He is choosing failure, as his brain and body are comfortable with it. Remember how the brain works? Because most of us do not have any experience with success or how to face our feelings, our brain creates the chemicals to keep us right where we are—homeostasis, reliving our worst day. Most people use shame, anger, and rejection to fuel them; then they make all this money, achieve all these things, have kids and the lifestyle they thought they wanted, and they are still miserable. They are hollow inside because they have used the wrong thing to fuel them. They have used anger and shame to drive them and that's a limited fuel source. That's why people experience midlife crises. They are actually running from their pain. They won't face it. And that's what is in front of you. You are about to face your trauma and actually step into your life and you are terrified.

Just What Is Success?

How do we define success? We have been told success is a thing, an achievement. I'd like to share my story of success with you. One day I was out for a bike ride and pulled up to a stoplight. I had my feet clipped into my pedals, so I unclipped my left foot waiting for the light to change. For some reason, I decided to shift my weight to my right foot and forgot I was clipped in on that side. I just fell over and trapped myself under my bike. I was like an octopus tangled in a tree in the middle of the intersection. I finally managed to get upright as the light was turning. I started pedaling and this massive feeling hit me. I realized that when I fell over, I didn't even consider what the people around me were thinking.

What do we typically do when we make an ass of ourselves? We feel shame and embarrassment and then we try to hide it. I understood the meaning of success when I realized I was completely humiliating myself without even recognizing it as humiliation—because I accepted who I was. For me, that's the true meaning of success. I went home and I looked up the definition of "success" in the dictionary and saw what I expected. Descriptions like affluence, achievement, and the accumulation of possessions. That's when I saw the Latin root of the word: "succedere." It means to come close after. That's when it hit me. We all have the wrong definition of success. The English dictionary has changed the original intent of this word and defined success as reaching somewhere or acquiring something outside of us, whereas the Latin root defines it as something we never arrive at it. We come closer but we never get there. It is a lifelong process. What I did when I fell over was get better. I got closer after humiliating myself. Success is ultimately self-acceptance of where we are inside ourselves at that moment.

Fear and Status

It's easy to compare ourselves to others. There are people who appear to be successful; they have the multimillion-dollar careers, the expensive vehicles, the massive homes, the massive 401Ks, and the best travel-filled Facebook posts. In my experience, these are the types of people who are the most filled with fear. I grew up in this kind of environment, a country-club lifestyle where families had their own private planes. Yet I was able to see through all of that. I saw the pain as a child, and I see it now. Money and possessions create a built-in denial system. We look at wealthy people and think, *They must have it all*. I can say without a doubt that the wealthiest are the ones in the most pain from the Worst Day Cycle. These people walk around all day scared to death of letting other people know how absolutely broken they feel inside. This is a massive fear-inducing situation.

What you have with affluence is the use of anger, shame, and denial to "succeed." It is incredibly rare to find anyone of affluence who hasn't suffered massive, unspeakable trauma that they have then stepped on and used like booster engines to acquire things—they are attempting to fill the hole created by the rejection, inadequacy, and powerlessness they suffered. This is why so many actors, athletes, and politicians have such problems with drugs, depression, and suicide issues. Fear is very powerful and it creates havoc when we don't know where it is coming from. No matter what our fears are, it's time to face them. In the next chapter, we'll see how shame gives us our power back. As exciting as this is, it puts us in a double bind.

> ## Your Journey to Success Steps
> 1. The first step in identifying fear is asking yourself the following questions, and then taking time to write down your responses in a journal or notebook or on the computer. (Keep in mind that, in some cases, fear is hidden so you may need to search for it until you find it.)
>   - Where and when did you feel rejected in your past?
>   - Where and when do you feel rejected currently?
>   - Where and when do you feel inadequate in your past?
>   - Where and when do you feel inadequate currently?
>   - Where and when do you feel powerless in your past?
>   - Where and when do you feel powerless currently?
>   - What has fear cost you?
>   - What do you do to medicate any of these fears away?
> 2. Once an hour, take a minute to listen to and feel your breath. Doing so shuts down your amygdala and quiets your brain.
> 3. Go to your feelings list and identify what you are feeling right now. If you are feeling anxious, write down those feelings in a journal or talk to a helping professional.
> 4. When you wake up each day, immediately write down three things you like about yourself. Don't overthink it. Just write it down.
> 5. Each evening, write down three things you accomplished that day. Even on your so-called worst day you'll realize you've accomplished a lot more than you think. This activity will prime your brain for the morning.

Chapter Six

Shame: The Silent Epidemic

We drop into shame due to the enormity of our feelings—namely, fear—induced by our original trauma. Shame is the feeling of having little-to-no self-worth. If we feel rejected, inadequate, and/or powerless, we conclude that something must be inherently bad or wrong with us. The other side of shame is that we use those negative feelings against ourselves to try to get our power back. Shame is all about control. Our power was taken from us during the original trauma, and shame is our way of taking it back. We gain control of others when we self-victimize by getting sick or hurt. We choose our careers, partners, and hobbies to set up our own failure and victimization. We do this because at least we are the ones doing it to ourselves. Until now, nobody taught us the skills we need to cope in healthy ways. It's time to release the shame and create the life we want. On this journey, we will discover that shame is a gift and not a curse.

That Dirty Little Secret

> *Shame is that feeling in the pit of your stomach that is dark as hell. You can't talk about it and you can't articulate how bad it feels because then everyone would know your "dirty little secret."*
> —Brené Brown, *I Thought It Was Just Me*

Shame is one of those universal emotions. Shame researcher Brené Brown refers to shame as the silent epidemic. She notes, "What makes it 'silent' is our inability or unwillingness to talk openly about shame and explore the ways in which it affects our individual lives, our families, our communities and society." Brown is right. We experience shame when we feel there is something wrong or bad about us. We typically don't talk about it with others. It truly becomes that "dirty little secret." People often confuse shame with guilt. Guilt is a bit different. Guilt is when we feel there is something wrong or bad about our behavior, but not that we are a bad person. Guilt leads us to look at a mistake, take ownership, and put a plan in place to do something differently. Very few people look at their imperfections that way. When we feel to the core that we are flawed, worthless, unimportant, and not good enough, these shameful feelings become self-talk that resembles, "I am so stupid, I'm such an idiot, what was I thinking?" These are words that match our feelings of worthlessness.

The Worst Day Cycle

Shame is the feeling of having little-to-no worth. We use it against ourselves to try to get our power back.

TRAUMA → FEAR → SHAME → DENIAL

Regaining Our Lost Power

To overcome that sense of worthlessness, we choose poor relationships, stagnant or unsatisfying careers, and even hobbies to hurt ourselves. We do so because it unwittingly gives us power. We can control these choices and others and thereby govern exactly how the trauma will happen. While we had no choice or control in the original trauma, this is our attempt to reconcile that power vacuum. I learned about the self-victimizing controlling-of-others piece of shame at a young age. After I found my mom passed out naked on the toilet when I was ten, I was in and out of hospitals with countless illnesses, injuries, broken bones, and stomach and back problems that doctors could never find a cause for. The last time my back went out, I was in the garage lying on the concrete floor. My crutches were in the rafters and I'm screaming at my mom to come help me. After yelling for several minutes, I finally shout, "You selfish son of a bitch, when are you going to stay sober long enough to take care of me?" I can still feel the chill that ran up my spine and the ice-cold realization that followed those words. As I lay there on the cold concrete, I realized this was the one and only time she was drunk when I was actually sick or hurt. I suddenly knew I had been making myself sick and hurt for years in an attempt to control her drinking.

It turns out I was controlling more than my mom with my sicknesses and injuries. I can still recall hearing the garage door close when my dad would come home from work. I can hear the one, two, three steps he would take through the laundry room and then the thirty or so feet he would walk through the kitchen, into the family room where I would be sick lying on the couch. I can still see his big smile, feel the strength of his hands as he would lean down, brush my hair back, and ask, "How are you doing, big guy?" This was the man who was so preoccupied trying to pay for all of our activities and who was struggling so much with his own demons that he had a hard time connecting or spending time with us. But when he got home from work, I owned him and that house. All of it revolved around Kenny and his illnesses. The other kids would get sick, but I was always the sickest. I made sure of it. That's what we all do. We victimize ourselves, and the greatest way to do that is to get sick or hurt. Since most of our life we have been firing the worst day chemical soup, our brain and body want more of it—we seek what we know. This means that stopping this self-victimization would create discomfort in our brain and body.

The Science Backs Up My Garage Floor Realization

As noted previously, the AMA states that 80 percent of all health problems are stress related (stress is fear), and even the conservative CDC acknowledges that 85 percent of all diseases have an emotional element.

The HeartMath Institute, a nonprofit research and education organization, has a mission of helping people of all ages reduce stress, self-regulate their emotions, and build energy and resilience for healthy, happy lives. One of the researchers at HeartMath, Lisa Hart-Wonton, looked at how our thoughts affect our health and well-being. She refers to the study Local and Non-Local Effects of Coherent Heart Frequencies on Conformational Changes of DNA to make her point. This study, conducted by Drs. Glen Rein and Rollin McCraty, found that thinking about and feeling anger, fear, and frustration actually causes our DNA to change shape in our bodies. In this particular study, twenty-eight vials of human placenta were given to twenty-eight researchers who were trained to feel both positive and negative feelings. When the researchers felt positive emotions like love, appreciation, and gratitude, the DNA relaxed; it unwound and became longer. When they switched their feelings to anger, fear, or frustration, the DNA tightened up; it became shorter. This research helps prove my point that how you feel has a direct impact on the life you choose to live.

According to Dr. Bruce Lipton, gene disorders like Huntington's chorea, beta thalassemia, and cystic fibrosis affect less than 2 percent of the population. This means the vast majority of the world's population comes into this world with genes that should allow them to live a happy and healthy life. He notes a staggering 98 percent of diseases are the result of lifestyle choices and, therefore, thinking. While Lipton uses the term "thinking," you may recall our thoughts are primarily dictated by what we *feel*. And those feelings from the Worst Day Cycle cause toxic shame.

Escaping the Cycle

My client Rose came to me for guidance because she was terrified of public speaking. She had consulted with several coaches but was still struggling with the fear. The standard suggestions around visualization, breath work, and positive self-talk just weren't working for her. They weren't fully dealing with what needed to be addressed. It's analogous to giving a patient an aspirin after open-heart surgery. Aspirin just isn't sufficient to address the pain.

As we discussed her feelings, I asked her, "When you think about that fear, when was the first time you felt that feeling?" She teared up and began recounting how her mother would physically abuse her and tell her she would amount to nothing. I asked her to pay attention over the next few days to what she was feeling and to what she does after having those feelings. I had told her about the shame portion of the Worst Day Cycle and that we unwittingly look for ways to re-create that trauma, fear, and shame. When she came back for our next session, she told me that she loves to read about history, especially World War II, and watch movies and documentaries about it. She is fascinated by the violence, the rape, the torture, and so forth. While she had just thought she just wanted to learn more about history, she now realized this interest went deeper—it was a way of reliving the abuse she suffered at the hands of her mother. Whenever she felt stress (which is fear), she would go on her computer and start reading or watching things about World War II. She is not alone here. Many people are drawn to horror movies and crime shows because they identify with these images and story lines. By watching these types of shows, which represent their trauma, they attempt to control their trauma and regain the power they lost when they first experienced it. Now they are the ones choosing the trauma. Just like Rose, most are completely unaware of their true motivations.

Be Cautious of Playing the Victim

My client Kelly was struggling in her real estate career. She complained that her boss was very inconsistent in regard to his expectations and the direction he wanted his agents to take. Each week he started a new initiative. Not seeing her part in the problem, she blamed the lack of productivity on her boss. She was being courted by other companies, but she just didn't feel like she could leave. Kelly also mentioned she was having a hard time dating. She had a fear of connecting, so she was resorting to drinking too much and having casual sex. Whenever she would start to develop a connection, she would pull away and start over with someone else. She was also struggling with smoking and binge eating because she felt so "stressed" by how everyone was treating her. Further, she confided that she had incredibly heavy and painful periods each month. While she had been to specialists, no one could figure out what was going on or how to relieve her pain. As we began the process of addressing her problems, it became very clear to me that Kelly was stuck in her Worst Day Cycle. Worse yet, her cycle moved fast, creating multiple opportunities for re-victimization.

Kelly is no different from the rest of us. Because we are unaware of how all of this works, we drop into the victimhood of the shame part of the cycle and then feel that our life would fall back into place—if only we could fix everyone around us. As I began to delve into each issue she was dealing with, I discovered that her mother was living with her because she had severe health issues. Just like her boss, her mother played helpless. Kelly mentioned how her siblings refused to help out with her mom. They were done with their mother's manipulations, but Kelly just couldn't turn her back on her or she would have nowhere to go.

She also disclosed her dad's rules when she was growing up: Rule #1: Psychology is for the weak minded. We are a tough family. Rule #2: We stick together no matter what. We are loyal to each other above all else. Eventually, Kelly divulged that her brother had exposed himself to her when they were kids. She completely shut down for two weeks, barely functioning when she recalled this incident as an adult. To her credit, she had made progress and did not return to casual sex or drinking. However, she did self-victimize through smoking and binge eating, bringing her to her heaviest weight ever. Throughout the process, Kelly had difficulties coming to our weekly sessions. There always seemed to be some catastrophe that made her cancel.

Kelly's story illustrates how the shame self-victimization process works.

Kelly herself was incredibly inconsistent in her life, so she selected a boss who matched the types of feelings she had about her mother. Both her mother and boss were draining her for support. Her boss was also just as dogmatic as her father. Her intense heavy periods were likely connected to the shame she felt over her brother's exhibitionist behavior. As Author Louise Hay points out, "Menstrual problems are the result of the rejection of one's femininity." Kelly acknowledged that she believed her genitals were sinful or dirty. She also ate heavily because, as she said, "If I'm fat, no one will sleep with me." When faced with difficulties, she shut down and became helpless just like her mother. She remarked, "There is this feeling that if I don't do all of these things for other people, I am somehow bad. Every time I think about taking care of me, this feeling comes up and it is so terrifying I run from it." That was her father. His demand for secrecy and loyalty created a mental and emotional prison that she was now voluntarily checking herself into.

Her work, relationships, and health were all showing her what her trauma and pain are. She is hurting herself with her choices and that is keeping her in pain. That is the blessing of the self-victimization piece of shame—if we are able to recognize it, then we can take action to change it. We are inflicting the pain to try to tell ourselves what our roadblocks are in the journey to success.

Our Parents' Role in Shame

As we discovered in chapter 4, many of us have been exposed to codependent and enmeshed parents. Our parents meant well but just didn't have the information. Do you recall Trish's email conversation with her parents? Her parents needed her to stay a child to keep her bond with them. She isn't aware of it, but subconsciously she believes that if she grows up and pursues her own dreams, she will lose her connection to them. She still struggles with the concept that her parents were anything but perfect, even after bringing me that email string. This is another devastating consequence of shame. We accept the false beliefs and ideas that our parents implanted in us. We have to "be" that person to keep our connection to them.

Another client, Lindsay, completely refused to let go of the false persona she had adopted to keep her connection with her parents. Therefore, she couldn't see that her relationship struggles were all her own doing. She recounted how the men she dated just were never ready for a relationship. They repeatedly lied about not being married, had never recovered from their divorce, or, after three or four dates, simply stopping calling or texting her.

When a client comes in with a laundry list of judgments, complaints, or things they hate in other people, I immediately recognize that they are telling me all about themselves. They are stuck in the shame and denial portions of the Worst Day Cycle and are completely unaware of it. For starters, Lindsay was consumed with taking care of her parents and was also playing a major role in raising her grandson. She told me she was raised to always put others first and not be selfish. I mentioned the concept of saying *no* and she physically withdrew from the idea. She said, "I could never do something like that; I would never be that mean and selfish." Finally, in our seventh session, she talked about her divorce for the first time. She said she had done everything for her husband and he still left. It was the first time in all of our sessions that the real Lindsay had shown up. She continued on about how divorce just wasn't acceptable in her family. The tears began to flow as we talked about how she had never grieved the divorce. She shared how her life since the breakup had been all about everyone but her. She didn't realize that she was selecting men who weren't available for a relationship because she wasn't ready either. In essence, she was still married to her ex-husband. She was beginning to see how her inability to find a relationship had everything to do with her. She had not dealt with her childhood or the divorce and it was getting in the way of her seeking new relationships.

I received a text from Lindsay the following day telling me how much she had learned in our last session. I replied, "I think it has been a very long time since someone has actually heard *you*!" I was hopeful we had turned the corner in dealing with her Worst Day Cycle. A common occurrence for clients who begin to release the worse day chemicals is they get sick. It is actually a great sign that they are letting go. She canceled the next week because she felt ill. Sadly, her health continued to deteriorate and she unexpectedly needed to have two surgeries. I have not seen her since. That is how powerful the Worst

Day Cycle can be. She just wasn't ready to sever the connection to her parents or to her ex-husband, and she was still not ready to "be nice" to herself.

Our Greatest Strength Gets Buried

As feelings of shame overwhelm us, we start believing those feelings. They become our identity and the "me" that we take out into the world. Once we have those false beliefs, we stick with them because they make us feel that we have control over other people's feelings and behavior. We are dead wrong. Ironically, this is what keeps us connected to the people who originally created that shame for us. Holding onto shame also shields us from other people's feelings and leaves us unable to connect with them because we don't want to feel; we don't want to risk being vulnerable. But the biggest reason we hang onto shame is because we get power from it when we revictimize ourselves. It's how we all attempt to reconcile the trauma that was passed down to us.

Sara was referred by the naturopath office that asked me to start seeing some of their clients who were stalling in getting their health back. For quite some time, Sara's doctor had suggested she come to see me but, as it is with most people, we won't address the pain until it is great enough. That pain finally reached a crisis point and that's when I first met Sara. At work, her new manager accompanied her on a sales call and it didn't go well. Wanting to express his new power, he was highly critical of how she went about her job. She had a complete emotional breakdown and then broke out with a case of shingles. According to author Louise Hay's symptom list, shingles is the result of waiting for the other shoe to drop, fear and tension, and being too sensitive. She took a medical leave and began working with me. I learned that Sara's father was highly critical of her. He never missed an opportunity to let her know he wished he had a son. As every child would do, Sara looked for every way possible to get her father's love.

She became a devoted and accomplished athlete, receiving a scholarship to run track. While at an out-of-state track meet in college, Sara agreed to leave the hotel one night with a friend who wanted to get some snacks. While on their snack run, the two young women were abducted and raped. (A side note: Sara repeatedly shared how she had a terrible time making decisions.

She said she would become flustered and just not know what to do. She wasn't sure where that came from. To address this, I used a technique called tapping, which often helps clients who are stuck in shame. It allows them to recall the event and feel it as intensely as possible and then share the emotions associated with it. Once they have shared this information, I begin tapping on specific points while I take the words they used. The idea behind it is that it breaks the subconscious connection to the event, thus freeing them of the trauma. It has been highly successful and it was with Sara as well.) As Sara talked about the feeling associated with the rape, she kept coming back to how she felt tremendous guilt for her decisions that day. She thought she could have done things differently or better. As she shared the events, she talked about how she spoke to the perpetrators, therefore making the two of them more human. She shared that her rape wasn't as brutal as her friend's and that, by talking to the abusers as humans, they eventually let them go. While tapping on the event, I drew on this. The truth was, Sara's greatest criticism of herself (the inability to make decisions) was her greatest strength. Had it not been for her choice to engage the abusers, their treatment could have been much worse. She not only loved herself and her teammate; in a sense she loved the abusers by allowing them to see their own humanness and pain.

In essence, Sara had been trapped in the Worst Day Cycle created by her father. To overcome that less-than-nurturing parenting, she had made an amazing choice. She decided that her only option to survive it was to become what her father wanted. Upon seeing these truths and her amazing decision-making skills, Sara was able to release the guilt, fear, and shame. Her shingles subsided and her manager began leaning on her to help him with the sales team. He values her insights and transformation. She can take his suggestions because she no longer sees them as criticism (her father) but instead as opportunities for growth. She can also recognize the unhealed issues that her manager is projecting, issues that often have nothing to do with her.

False Mantras and Self-Talk

A hallmark of the shame piece of the cycle are the mantras and destructive self-talk we use to self-victimize. Sara's "I don't make good decisions," Lindsay's "I'm too nice," and my own mantras of "What's the point?" or "It just doesn't matter" are key ingredients and insights we need to become aware of and deal with to overcome our shame. We all have some kind of mantra we play over and over again. It gives us permission to not confront an issue in our life.

We all have a responsibility to ourselves as victims. My counselor told me this story to help illustrate the point. He shared,

> "Imagine you are walking down the street and you are shot by a sniper. The bullet came out of nowhere. You didn't do anything wrong, but you got shot. There you are on the concrete with a bullet in your leg. It's unfair that you got shot—you didn't deserve it; you didn't do anything to bring that on. This person made that choice. But as you lie there on the concrete, you still have a choice. You can choose to bleed out and scream about how awful you have been treated and how unfair it is. You can choose to stay the victim and die on that sidewalk. Or you can use whatever ability you have in that leg, along with the rest of your body, to get yourself to the hospital and get that bullet taken out. It's up to you."

Just getting to the hospital is not enough. Now that you have realized that you have this bullet in your leg, it's not over when the bullet is taken out. It's up to you to choose to go to physical therapy to rebuild the muscles and regain the ability to walk. That's a great metaphor for all of this trauma work, especially the self-victimizing shame portion. None of us deserves to be shot by the sniper we were all wounded by. Our parents were shot by it, their parents were shot by it, and we've been shot by it. None of us are to blame; we didn't do anything wrong. But now we have this bullet in our leg. What society and the Worst Day Cycle has taught us is to stay lying on the concrete and bring everyone else into it.

The Power of Self-Victimization

Self-victimization works because it gives us the power we lost in our original trauma, returning that power in two ways. First, we gain false power by inadvertently controlling the actions and feelings of those around us through our health conditions and our personal and professional struggles. Second, we gain power because we are doing it to ourselves. As noted previously, it's like the newly divorced person who goes out drinking and sleeping around, thinking, "I'll show them!" They intentionally hurt themselves, but at least they are doing it to themselves. Choosing to inflict pain on ourselves comes from the false belief system created by shame. It is an attempt to lessen the powerful feelings of rejection, inadequacy, and powerlessness we feel from not being able to control the other person. If you aren't ready to accept that you are subconsciously bringing on the maladies in your life just yet, then keep going. I will go into this "opposite" mindset in the next chapter on denial, where we will learn why we deny these truths about ourselves and how this denial re-creates our trauma and spurs us right back to the top of the Worst Day Cycle. Don't give up yet. By having that information, coupled with what we've learned so far, you will have all of the tools necessary to continue your journey to success.

> ### Your Journey to Success Steps
> 1. Drop out of denial and realize that you are hurting yourself and that any problem is your own creation.
> 2. Become an expert in how you are doing that and find out how you created a false persona during your initial trauma.
> 3. Look at how you are holding onto that false persona to keep your connection with your original perpetrators.
> 4. Discover the mantras you are using against yourself and develop healthier, more empowering mantras.

Chapter Seven

The Trap of Denial

Denial can be a lifesaver for a period of time. It protects us from the original intense feelings of the trauma we've endured and creates a buffer that allows us time to absorb the full weight of the experience. Sadly, we are not taught how to revisit this denial. Therefore, I believe it is the single greatest killer in society today. By not returning to it, our self-victimization continues. In turn, this spurns the next revolution in the Worst Day Cycle. We deny, suppress, repress, and minimize our trauma to preserve our self-concept. Since we have become the trauma, that is the only "me" we know. To give that up would feel like the death of who we are. It leaves the question, "If this self-concept isn't me, then who am I?" We also hold onto it because we had to adapt to it to keep our connection to our caregivers. It's easy to believe, "If I give up these beliefs, in effect, I am severing the only connection I have to my parents/caregivers." That's a tough pill to swallow.

This is essentially where our fear of success is born. We believe, "If I succeed, I will be losing my connection to my adaptive self but, more importantly, to my caregivers." We're angry inside because we don't know how to face our denial. This shows up as judgment, projection, criticizing, blaming, and hating others. The beauty of all this is that our hidden anger is a window into ourselves, our self-victimization, and our Worst Day Cycle. Anything we hate, judge, criticize, blame, and project upon is always about us. We only see these things in others because they are operating in us. We are screaming our Worst Day Cycle out loud in the hopes we will finally hear ourselves. It is our intense feelings and the choices we make to avoid them that trigger new trauma, so we once again repeat the cycle.

The Worst Day Cycle

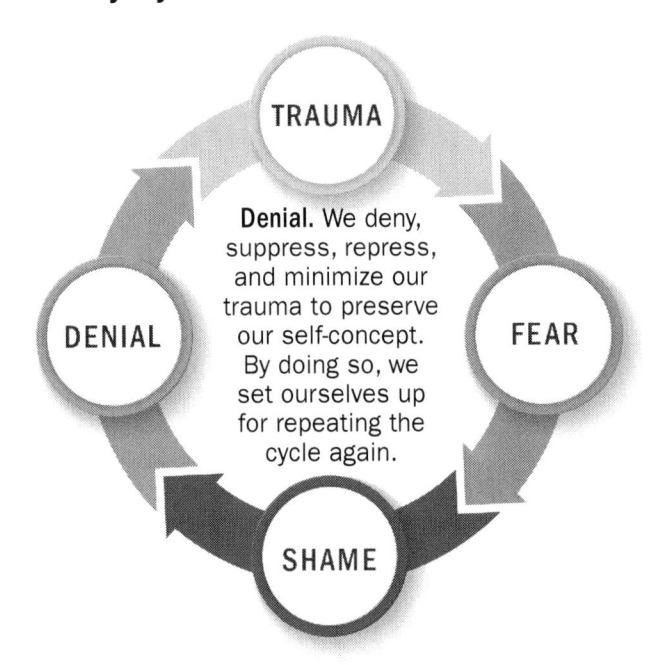

```
        TRAUMA
   ↗              ↘
DENIAL          FEAR
   ↖              ↙
        SHAME
```

Denial. We deny, suppress, repress, and minimize our trauma to preserve our self-concept. By doing so, we set ourselves up for repeating the cycle again.

The Deal about Denial

Denial keeps us in our Worst Day Cycle in four ways:

1. We had to adopt a false self-concept to keep our connection to our caregivers, who provided either abusive or less-than-nurturing parenting. To drop that concept feels like the death of the "me" we know.
2. Since that false concept is our only connection to them, to drop that connection leaves us feeling like we have no parents. We are afraid we will then be completely alone in the world.
3. We then hate, judge, blame, criticize, and project upon other things in our life. This is always a direct reflection of aspects of ourselves we have not dealt with or dislike.

4. By not addressing the above three issues, we suffer new trauma and start the cycle all over again.

For instance, I have a client who recently dropped out of denial regarding her role in the family. She had been feeling and doing wonderfully. She came into my office leaking tears and feeling frustrated, and she had no idea why. Mary's role growing up was to be the support for her parents. Her father used to say, "You're the one I never have to worry about." This essentially meant he never had to invest in her and he never did. He went to everyone else's games and events but not hers. Mary had also just set a boundary with her toxic mother, who responded by saying, "I don't even know you anymore. Don't you know you're supposed to take care of your mother?" Mary had never been able to live her life. It was always about feeding her parents' needs—playing the role of parent to them. This is who she "is." Everyone has an adapted false concept. I am nice, I am sarcastic, I am quiet, I am loud, I am shy, I am… and the list goes on. In almost all cases, that false self is working against us—not for us—just like it was with Mary. Realizing she had spent her life and her current career taking care of everyone but herself, to give that up feels devastating. Walking away from that role and the false connection she had to her parents is the biggest and most painful step. It's like a personal death of herself and a move that feels tremendously isolating.

Our subconscious thought becomes, "If I stop this Worst Day Cycle, I will be alone in the world." The reality is that Mary has been alone all of her life. By stepping out of her false roles, she is no longer enabling her parents and, therefore, is creating the first real chance of forming a true connection with her parents and herself. It was her avoidance that was causing her pain. No matter what she did or accomplished, she always felt hollow inside. To compensate, she overworked, selected drug-addicted partners, and filled her schedule with to-do items. This is the case for all of us. We need to drop out of this denial if we want to feel satisfied with any of our accomplishments. This is the most difficult part of overcoming the Worst Day Cycle because it is so counterintuitive to everything we have ever experienced or been taught.

In *The Brain That Changes Itself*, Norman Doidge discusses neural plasticity, where social rigidity comes from, and why change is so difficult. He cites psychiatrist Bruce Wexler, a researcher from Yale University, who argues in his book *Braining Culture* that the relative decline in neural plasticity as we age explains many social phenomena. In childhood, our brains readily shaped themselves in response to the world and developed neuropsychological structures, which include our pictures or representations of the world. These structures form the neuronal basis for all of our perceptual habits and beliefs, all the way up to complex ideologies. Like all plastic phenomenon, the structures tend to get reinforced early on, if repeated, and become self-sustaining. As we age and plasticity declines, it becomes increasingly difficult for us to change in response to the world, even if we want to. We find familiar types of stimulation pleasurable, like seeking out like-minded individuals to associate with. Research shows we tend to ignore or forget, or attempt to discredit, information that does not match our beliefs and our perception of the world. This is because it is very distressing and difficult to think about and view the world in unfamiliar ways. This all helps explain why denial is so difficult to address. It is quite possible that many of you reading this are having that exact same experience now. This "information" does not match your lifelong rigid beliefs, so it will be instinctual to discredit it.

A Game-Changing New Perspective

I was in denial for decades and kept reliving that Worst Day Cycle. That was until I discovered the work of speaker and author Byron Katie. In my opinion, she is one of the best authorities on denial. After my second marriage ended, I had this unquenchable thirst to figure out why I kept ending up in the same place. I couldn't escape the memory of my wife and the feeling that overwhelmed me as a result. Repeatedly reliving my worst day was killing my soul and sending me on a chase I could never stop. I found much-needed clarity with Katie's method of self-inquiry, called "The Work." She asks clients to write down their stressful thoughts on paper and then answer the following questions:

- Is it true?
- Can you absolutely know it's true?

- What happens when you believe that thought?
- Who would you be without that thought?

While I recognized the value of asking those questions and use this method with my own clients, my favorite portion of The Work is where Katie does a turnaround that allows her clients to look at the situation from an exactly opposite point of view. And when it is done correctly, it can provide answers on how to get out of dire situations. I call this process "flipping it." I have yet to find a better method that confronts and reconciles denial better than her method. In one of her videos, *He Won't Forget the Past,* Katie meets with a woman whose fiancé called off their wedding. Through the self-inquiry process, the woman cleared up her confusion about staying stuck in the past. When she discovered the truth, instead of her story about it, her shame and anger turned into laughter. You can see the transformation in her face and body on the video. For the very first time, she saw herself for what she was—and she was able to love who she was.

My first wife and I fought for years during and after our marriage. I felt she had done me wrong and, although I thought I had dealt with my side of the street, I still had elements of anger and resentment toward her. By watching that Byron Katie video, I was able to see the final vestiges of my denial. I finally admitted that my wife gave me the exact treatment I felt I deserved and wanted. She had loved me perfectly based on my level of imperfection and brokenness. With this realization, I felt tremendous sadness for having manipulated her and basically teaching her it was okay to treat me that way. Of course, she was angry with me. Who would want a husband to manipulate the anger out of them the way I did? That video freed me. I instantly gained a new level of appreciation and care for her. If anyone asks me about my first wife today, I say, "I absolutely adore her." My resentment and anger toward her have left me. The video taught me why we all get stuck in not being able to forgive someone. I could not forgive my former wife because I could not forgive myself or see my denial. I wasn't angry at her; I was angry at myself. Once I saw me, I could forgive me. Like it or not, a lack of forgiveness comes from not dealing with our denial. We are still blaming someone else for our own shortcomings. We do this in part because we get so much out of being the victim, as we learned in the chapter on shame.

What Are We Getting from This?

One of my Realtor clients used to be very successful and then suddenly was not. He was living with his girlfriend and had no clients. He was struggling, as he felt he was a victim in this situation. Our conversation went something like this:

What are you getting from this situation?
Nothing. I hate this. I have no money.
How do you spend your day?
I get up, watch TV, lie on the couch, and hang out with my dog and sometimes go for a walk.
Who pays the bills?
She does.
Did you hear what you just said?

He looked at me with a blank stare. Although he didn't realize it at first, he got to do whatever he wanted and was provided with the added bonus of blaming others in the process. With this newfound knowledge, he was given a choice. He could accept that he actually had a great situation—he had no responsibility; it was like he was retired. The difficulty was that living this way went against his morals and values, and that is why he could not enjoy the freedom he had. Now that he was not in denial and was in reality, he could learn to stay in his current situation or he could do something about it. Blaming somebody else was no longer an option.

I told him to ask himself some questions now that he realized he wasn't a victim. Here are the questions and his answers to them:
- What am I getting from this?
  Freedom, no responsibility, and attention.
- Why am I doing this to myself?
  Because I'm afraid to succeed.
- What does this remind me of?

> *This reminds me of when my dad used to throw things at me and I felt frozen and stuck. I couldn't move.*

- What are my needs and wants?
  I want to be successful and have financial security.
- What's the smallest step I can take to get where I want to be?
  I can print out thirty real estate flyers and put them outside people's doors in the neighborhood.
- What did you accomplish today?
  I printed and distributed thirty flyers and sat and thought about what was going on with me.

This exercise helped him realize that his wants and needs conflicted with his action. That's when he knew he needed to make a change. So, the first step in getting unstuck in the denial portion of the Worst Day Cycle is to ask yourself, "What am I getting from this?" Like it or not, everyone has something they are getting out of staying in denial. When people are given the tools to look at their situation in a different light, they can take steps to transform their lives. Looking at it from the opposite viewpoint is a great start.

My client Ann has a type-A personality—she's someone who goes after what she wants. Her husband is an alcoholic who refuses to work because he is always pursuing the next big dream. He says he wants to go to motivational seminars and research his next move, but he is not moving. During our sessions, Ann disclosed that she had already made a plan for what they were going to do when they lost their home: move into a dinky apartment, with everything in storage because of him. She was becoming furious with him. During her ninth session with me, I flipped it around and said, "Look at what you're getting from this situation. You are setting up a construct where you are paying for your husband to go to these motivational seminars to learn how to be great. He says he wants to go and then he'll figure his life out. But nothing is happening." If her husband never works and they lose everything, then she can say, "See, this is your fault." She had essentially decided to sacrifice her career, lifestyle, and goals just so she could poke him in the chest and say that. She had set up a dynamic and perpetrated it so she could play the victim and blame him. The problem was not her husband—it was the opposite. She was in denial that she was playing an equal, if not bigger, piece in both of them playing out their Worst Day Cycles. How content we are in our life is directly correlated to how much denial we have worked through. The more miserable our life is, the more denial we are in. That has been my experience personally and with every client I've worked with. Once we confront our denial, happiness awaits on the other side. Unearthing that denial can be difficult. But we need to be willing to do the work.

The Power of Denial

Denial is pervasive in our everyday lives. "Stress" is the popular buzzword, right? Limit stress, lower your stress, I am so stressed… Remember what stress is? When we talked about fear, I pointed out how the stress reaction is the fear reaction. When we are in "stress," we are in white-hot fear. But, we can't say I am afraid; that would make us too vulnerable and real and make us sound weak. So instead, we go into massive denial and create a false word to ignore the real problem.

If I say I am stressed, what does that really communicate?
- I must be meditating and reading every day for three hours.
- I must be working out two hours a day, six days a week.
- I need to work 6 a.m. to 8 p.m., but I take time away to volunteer in my child's class for three hours at a time.
- I must be on every committee to promote my kids.
- Because I am so good at all of this, I am also learning how to dance, sing, paint, play an instrument, travel the globe, and fix world hunger—but just as a hobby.

In other words, we are shouting, "I am stressed because I am doing so much more than you." Denial like this allows us to ignore the real issue and keeps us perpetrating our own self-abuse while we project onto, judge, and blame others.

I was at the Starbucks in Sedona and there were zip ties holding up outdoor lights on a metal railing on the patio. As I sat there, I watched a young lady walk right up to the rail and scrape her arm against the nub of a zip tie. Immediately, she talked about being afraid it might bleed. She stood there looking at her arm, squeezing it, and waiting for it to bleed. Although there was no blood, her boyfriend and another friend began talking about how dangerous it was to have those zip ties holding up the lights. They went inside to complain.

I was shocked at the lack of their own personal responsibility for what had happened and their complete denial. Instead of taking responsibility for her actions, this woman expected somebody else to do it for her. I ended up watching the shame, self-victimization, and denial portions of the Worst Day Cycle happen right in front of my eyes. No one did anything to her; she hurt herself, co-opted her friends into rescuing her, and then dropped into denial that she had any responsibility for her actions. The three of them were completely unaware of what they had just done to themselves. Sadly, within thirty minutes a maintenance man arrived to cut down the lights to avoid a potential lawsuit from a professional victim stuck in denial and living in her Worst Day Cycle. This mindset of self-victimization and denial is limited and contingent upon somebody else rescuing us and being responsible for our life. When our survival, happiness, peace, and safety depend on somebody else, we are destined to live a life where we are scared to death and therefore feel inadequate.

Jay's story is an excellent example of the power of denial and how we constantly replay the movie of our trauma in an effort to see and deal with our pain. When Jay was a child, his family moved to a new city and it traumatized him. He went from having lots of friends and fitting in to having no friends and not fitting in. His defense mechanism for that pain was to always have, as he said, "an exit strategy." But, as we do when we have been traumatized, we also create ways to stay in the trauma. As crazy as it sounds, his way of staying stuck was by holding onto an antique armoire. As we worked toward him facing his denial, this "piece" of furniture came up. Pay attention to the words he used to describe it. Jay started telling me how his first memory of the armoire was that it "didn't fit" in the moving van, so it was "alone" and "separate" from everything else and "strapped" to the top of the car. He didn't know why he had been "lugging" it around for years. He shared, "I have 'spent' thousands of dollars moving it all across the country. It has become like a 'coffin' I just can't get out of, and whenever I contemplate leaving a situation, I always have to take into consideration the 'cost' and the 'hassle' of taking this piece with me. It has become this 'anchor' that keeps me 'stuck.'"

As I listened, I was completely floored by what he had just told me but, more important, how he didn't even hear himself. He had no connection to the power and metaphor of his own words and life story. He was separate from his own existence. Every day, in idle conversation, I hear people express this type of pain. Unbeknownst to them, they are telling us exactly what is keeping them from what they want. When my clients learn how the cycle operates in their life, they begin to hear it in others also. Everyone talks this way. He wants to leave, he wants to pick someone who is actually present in his life, but the trauma from his past won't allow it. So, he selects yet another lover or business partner who will leave him "strapped to a car" and outside of the collective van, which is his metaphor for his full self. His lack of information on trauma, fear, shame, and denial has him re-creating the cycle repeatedly. This is what keeps us from the success we want in all areas of our life.

The armoire (his pain) is a part of the caravan; it follows along but it is always separate and alone. Furthermore, it is "tied" to the journey. It can't be disengaged and allowed to go in a different direction. So, he wakes up one day and contemplates leaving but the "cost," the "size," and the "weight" of moving that *huge* piece of furniture is too much. Dealing with his original abandonment and pain is too much. It is an anchor that keeps him stuck. The thought of leaving means he has to, literally and figuratively, reattach and grab that anchor of pain, the pain he has left submerged below the surface, while he endured newer pain with this new lover or business partner. If he does move, he just relocates on to the same place because he still has that original "antique." His pain is now older, more chiseled and frayed, and in many ways more precious. It has become his memory "chest" that stores his years of hurt. As he shared his story, here is what I heard: "I am the armoire! You, Kenny, are asking me to auction off the one thing that has been with me and that I have been able to count on for my whole life. I trust this pain; I know that no matter what, it can be strapped to a car and come with me when none of the people in my life would do that—not even my parents. Fuck you for asking me to give up the only thing that I have been able to count on."

I walked Jay through his actual words as it became apparent that the armoire kept him anchored to his trauma. I asked, "Did you hear the words you chose when you told me your story?" He did not. I asked him to think about it. I wanted him to find the answer on his own. As I talked to him, I guided him into his own denial and self-victimization. As I asked the questions, Jay appeared disoriented. Then his face changed and he was like, "OMG, the armoire is my trauma I've been carrying all of these years." And then the real work started to happen. I told him, "Look, be kind to yourself; you didn't know. Now that you do, you can start to forgive yourself. That is when change happens." He hated himself for carrying this pain around for years and now that he has actually seen it, he can actually accept who he is. Now he is looking at the trauma of moving around as a kid and he's seeing the reality. He is essentially loosening the straps on the car holding the armoire, which represents the false self he had to create.

Denial is like that weight of the armoire for Jay. Essentially, we are saying, "Please don't make me face my pain. I have no skills or tools to handle this overwhelming sense of inadequacy and rejection, so I need you to carry the weight, to pay the freight on my pain." Just like Jay's coffin metaphor, we are all trapped by the emotions stemming from our Worst Day Cycle. When we learn to listen for it, we hear the pain and torture that shows up in every aspect of our life.

The True Meaning of Judgment, Criticism, Blame, Projection, and Hate

One of my clients is divorced. She shared a text message she received from her ex-husband following her father's funeral, where she gave the eulogy. Please note what I'm about to share is the first part of the actual text message. I will then show you what is really being said by flipping the statement around. This provides a window into all of our denial.

> It's just like you to start an argument and not listen; it's all about you. You need to hear the truth but you can't. You talk about your new truth but it's in your head, not reality. I hope it helps you get away from those new-age gurus and head healers you listen to and off the countless meds and drugs you need to cope.

It's just like me to start an argument and not listen; it's all about me. I need to hear the truth but I can't. I talk about your new truth but it's in my head, not reality. I hope it never helps you get away from those new-age gurus and head healers you listen to and off the countless meds and drugs you need to cope.

> And there is one more thing I need to say since we are cleansing and being honest. I was a great man before I met you and you just wore me down! You were a head case when I met you and you always will be. You are the most emotionally self-centered person I have ever met. No one can have a thought that does not match yours.

And there is one more thing I need to say since we are not cleansing and not being honest. I was not a great man before I met you and I just wore you down! I was a head case when you met me and I always will be. I am the most emotionally self-centered person you have ever met. No one can have a thought that does not match mine.

> Your speech at your dad's service was such a joke! Not about him at all…just about you!! "I saved my mom's life," "I saved my daughter's life," "I saved my dad's life!!" "Everyone is so lucky to have me in their life!!" It was so self-centered and self-serving. A definite only-child, I'm-the-center-of-the-world type of speech!

Your speech at your dad's service was not a joke! Not about him at all.

When I spoke to my client after she shared the text messages, my first question was, "What are your thoughts about it?" She began by explaining what happened at the funeral. As she stumbled for her words, she said, "Well, I called my girlfriends and they said it was great."

Her immediate defensiveness showed me her ex was correct and where she was in denial. It was in the unintentional self-serving nature of her speech and it was the most fact-laden portion of the whole text. The rest was just his emotional dislike for himself that he was projecting onto her.

When somebody is immediately defensive, typically it is because you are bringing up something that is true. Look for that reaction in yourself to begin addressing your own denial.

Unmasking Denial: An Opportunity to Quit Traumatizing Ourselves

Here's something to realize about denial: As we begin to address it and quit retraumatizing ourselves by living in the worst day, our brains develop new pathways, kind of like that sled I referred to in the fresh snow. Going down a path that others have never gone down can be rocky. When I started making these changes in my own life, my memory and even my ability to speak suffered. I still struggle with that at times. The first video I ever did on my YouTube channel took me six hours to make. I literally could not remember anything I wanted to talk about. Eventually, I had to write a whole story onto cue cards and hang them from the ceiling and position the camera so you couldn't tell I was reading from them. Everything gets disoriented as we "pull all the wires" out of the worst day of our life and begin repositioning those wires into our best day. This is normal and very much a part of the process. We might need to sleep more, cry more, be forgetful, mix our words up, and feel confused in many ways. That is a sign that everything is getting better. Just keep going. The greatest gift that comes from seeing our denial is that we also see our darkness. Before we can fully move out of our Worst Day Cycle, we need to examine our darkness and discover that what we view as our darkness is actually the opposite—it is our light. We will begin to do this in the following chapter.

> **Your Journey to Success Steps**
>
> 1. Watch the YouTube video, *He Won't Forget the Past* by Byron Katie.
> 2. In any situation you are in, ask yourself, "What am I getting from this?" Your answer will reveal the opposite of what you had previously thought.
> 3. Make a list of all the things in your life that you judge, criticize, or hate. More often than not, what you dislike in others has a lot to do with yourself. Go to Byron Katie's website, thework.com, and print out the *Judge-Your-Neighbor Worksheet* to help you recognize some of these same traits in yourself.

Chapter Eight

The Day I Saw My Darkness

I met a woman at a networking event and we decided to meet at Starbucks one afternoon to talk about our businesses. I asked her only two questions and she completely fell apart within the first five minutes of our meeting. When we sat down, I said, "So tell me more about you." She started to share the struggles she was wrestling with in her business and personal life. I could feel the pain in her. When she started to lose steam, I asked, "Do you have a history of people not seeing you or understanding what is really going on inside?" That's when she crumbled. She was sobbing as she talked about how broken she felt. I listened to her story and after about ninety minutes, we went our separate ways.

Our Darkness Is Our Power

Later that night, I went for a walk and I was feeling incredible. Looking over my day and the previous several months, I was beginning to see all of these positive changes in me. Finally, I was experiencing wonderful moments of insight and clarity. Opportunities were beginning to come my way. As I walked, I thought back on my conversation with this woman. I was feeling so good about how I could meet somebody and in a short period of time get them to be that vulnerable with me. Admittedly, I was feeling a bit smug thinking about what a gift I had and how people seemed to just open up so easily with me. I casually asked myself, "Why do you like what you do so much?" I heard the word "power" in my response. That startled me a bit, so I dug deeper and asked, "What do you like about power?" My next response changed my life, "It gives me power."

As I said those words, I felt this tremendous shuddering ache run through me, a feeling I now refer to as "shame burbs." I buckled at the knees and bent over. I had never been more present at feeling my emotions at this level of intensity. That's when it hit me. My darkness was power. Like a vampire, I had sucked the complete emotional life out of this woman for my benefit. I remember seeing the vacant look on her face as she left the coffee shop. I had not helped her—I had stolen from her. A soul-crushing darkness overtook me as I saw the devil in me. I saw the deepest, darkest part of myself that I never knew existed. I always viewed myself as a nice person who cared about others. I thought I was helping them. Now I realized it was for my selfish benefit. I was stunned and didn't know what to do with this realization. Then, almost as quickly as that darkness overtook me, pure light began seeping in and filled me. I felt at peace. This whole process happened in the span of about two seconds. It was a massive flooding of insight, delivered at hyper speed.

That experience shed so much light on why women leave me in relationships, why I can't keep friends, and why I would be ostracized by my teammates when I played hockey. I saw how my "niceness" wasn't nice at all. It was a manipulative power grab. I was stealing from people. For the first time, I could see that side of myself and how it operates. More important, now that I was aware, I could stop it. When I saw that, all of my shame and self-hatred left me. It was my inability to see all of me that had been destroying me and keeping me in the Worst Day Cycle. I was creating my own self-hatred because, until that point, I wasn't willing to face my denial about this part of me. Now I was overcome with self-forgiveness, and I could let that self-hatred go and escape this cycle. I know all of me now—the good, the bad, and the ugly. As my counselor taught me years ago, you cannot be blamed for something you don't know. I now saw the devil inside me. It helped me understand why I was so attracted to my second wife and why I married her. When I first saw her, I had the most surreal experience. We were about to have our first date and I was waiting for her outside the restaurant. As I turned my head, I could see her sauntering toward me about twenty feet away. I physically felt my body push back and I heard myself say, "Oh my God, she's the devil." What used to perplex me was now clear. The only reason I saw her as the devil was because I saw myself in her. I was the devil, not her. I was drawn and attracted to her because I needed her to show me how to bring out the deepest, darkest, most manipulative, destructive pieces of myself. And she did.

Seeing Our Darkness Leads to Forgiveness

The clarity continued over the weeks and months that followed. Just like an athlete who practices to become better and more precise at their sport, I went through a similar process when looking at my darkness. I became attuned to the often-subtle ways I self-victimize and manipulate others and how I drop into denial. I became aware of all my addictions, manipulations, and how I used people to feel good about myself. Instead of shame, I felt instant joy and forgiveness. I no longer need to be ashamed of my past or how this darkness operates in me. I've accepted it so it can no longer hurt me.

Forgiveness is why we need to go toward our darkness. Until we see all of ourselves—our perfect imperfections—we can't fully forgive ourselves. When we are criticized because of the Worst Day Cycle and our fear of success, our natural reaction is to drop into denial and defend ourselves. But when we stop that automatic reaction and instead turn toward the criticism, something amazing happens. When we discover our denial that hides in the darkness, it loses its power. When we forgive ourselves, others can't hurt us with it anymore. The feeling is incredibly freeing. As painful as it may seem, we must go right to our self-victimizing shame and especially our denial to find freedom. It's time to expose those imperfect, broken parts of ourselves and stop running away and hiding them from everyone. That is what is killing us. Every experience, good or bad, is an opportunity to learn about our darkness and imperfections. Our gift to ourselves, our children, our friends, and the world sits inside that part of us that we haven't been willing to look at.

The focus on our darkness is intentionally placed as a later chapter in this book because we need to be well along in our journey to begin to understand it. If I had discussed the topic at the beginning of the book, you might have rejected the concept and considered it too confrontational. It is my hope that by now our brains are acclimated enough to the new concepts that we can accept that we all have this darkness inside us, and it doesn't make us bad. Our darkness keeps us stuck in the Worst Day Cycle. In fact, our darkness is the cycle. Imagine what it would look like to go from darkness into light. By admitting our darkness and going toward it, we can find the light on the other side and that's when we fire our best-day chemicals. It's not easy to do, because our darkness is something we hide from everybody, even ourselves. There is tremendous darkness around our imperfections and around the trauma we've been through. We don't want to admit that. We'll go to great lengths to hide that.

Recognizing My Own Darkness

Now when that darkness shows up, I can do something about it. At the end of my presentations, I typically have a question-and-answer period. In a recent presentation, after a few questions were asked, a woman in the audience began telling the whole room how she was hurt as a child. The topics I spoke of that day had hit a chord. She explained that she had done a lot of work on her trauma but not much in the area of the self-victimizing shame or the denial portion. These are topics that, frankly, very few presenters ever touch on because we all chase the "feel good" stuff. She shared that she selected men who were abusive to her and then abandon her, that her most recent boyfriend had even told her right from the beginning that he would leave her. Yet she stayed and he kept his promise. She felt like she was a magnet, pulling these type of men toward her, and she wanted to know why. She was becoming emotional and she wanted to dig into the shame and denial and get some real relief and answers right then and there.

In that moment, as I stood on that stage, I saw my darkness. It comes from the right side. I heard thoughts like, "This is great; here's a chance to show everyone how gifted you are. You can completely expose her right in front of everyone with just a few simple questions. This will lead to a bunch of new clients when they see what you can do." There was this electricity that coursed through my body as I considered this opportunity. But instead of further exposing this woman and gaining power and admiration for myself, I pushed those thoughts away and told myself, "No, that's about you and your own pain. You no longer need to hurt yourself or her with it." I then proceeded to corral her emotionally. I pulled up a chair right in front of her instead of standing over her. She was seeing me as an authority and was emotionally putting herself under me. She was doing that because she saw I had that darkness in me, just like her abusers had. She was drawn to it and wanted to relive it through me. I had to physically get at her level so she could feel equal. I also had to break the cycle that we both shared—me as the abuser and her as the victim.

I told her that the topics she wanted to go into were very deep and that in this environment I would only be hurting her if we discussed them. Her desire to expose herself this publicly told me that she had a history of being horrifically shamed in public or at the very least in front of others. She didn't realize it, but I did. She wanted to relive it and I wasn't going to let her do that to herself. I wasn't going to do that to myself anymore, either. I told her, "This isn't a safe environment for you to expose yourself. If you open this up, I won't have enough time to help you through it." I knew it wouldn't be right of me to leave her fractured.

I was emotionally setting boundaries for her and slowly placing a barrier around her pain so she could gather herself back into that. I told her if she wanted to explore those things we could do it, but she would need to make an appointment with me in my office. I then gave her a few simple basic suggestions on how she could begin addressing her feelings of shame. This included stating three things she liked about herself in the morning, three things she accomplished in the evening, and looking in the mirror and telling herself, "I love you." I also asked her to look at what she was getting from picking the men she did. "There is a payoff for you; go find out what it is." She had stopped crying, she was back in herself, and at that point it became appropriate for me to stand back up.

Why We Need to Pursue Our Darkness

Our darkness is a metaphor for our imperfections. It is a by-product of the trauma and the imperfect nature of how we have all adapted to try to deal with our trauma. Having darkness does not make us bad. In fact, it is just as beautiful as our light. It gives birth to our light. We are all taught to just be positive and deny, ignore, stuff, repress, and suppress anything negative about ourselves. Herein lies the problem. We have all been hurt and in that moment of hurt we develop a coping skill that allows us to survive. But as we age, that way of coping usually works against us. We need to work through that. We've been told the past is the past, which is true, but we never completely leave the past. We just re-create it until we find the darkness in it.

It was not until I sat in deep critical thought about my darkness over a period of time, when I became an expert on my own denial, that I discovered how manipulative and ugly I can be. But look at the blessings of my darkness. I have insights and wisdom I can share that could have only come from my darkness. Like it or not, we all try to hide our darkness. Our self-worth is tied to how others view us. We might judge our worth through how many Facebook likes or comments we receive. Success is elusive, as we are taught it's all about money and status. If that's the case, why are so many of us walking around feeling so hollow inside?

As I observe people behaving imperfectly, instead of judging them as bad I see unreconciled trauma, fear, shame, and denial. What I see is me. If I no longer hate myself, I can't hate you. When I walked into my counselor's office for the first time fifteen years ago, he asked me what brought me there. I began to describe how I had disappointed myself in my marriage. I said, "I don't know how to be a man. I need to learn how to be a man." His reply would send me on a lifelong quest to be a better person, recognize what my true problems are, and discern where I sometimes get stuck in the cycle. He said, "Well, Kenny, when I was in your shoes, I went and became an expert on what my problems were." Those words stuck with me. As my life evolves, I gain a deeper appreciation for what he was actually saying.

Quit Running from Our Darkness

The following questions will help you continue to confront your denial and get an honest picture of yourself. Ask yourself the following questions:

- Is what I am doing working? (Ask this question in relation to your spouse, kids, health, friends, family, hobbies, and career.)
- If you answered yes, is that your denial? Are you truly satisfied, or is there fear in confronting the feelings of the Worst Day Cycle that compel you to say *yes*?
- How much will it cost me emotionally, spiritually, professionally, and relationally if I continue to ignore my darkness?
- Looking forward one, five, or ten years from now, am I willing to continue paying the price I have paid by avoiding my darkness?

For some of us, the answer will still be *yes*, we are willing to ignore it and continue to pay the price. That is fine, as I have done that, too. My suggestion, then, is to escalate all of our denial techniques. Instead of learning more about our emotions, our Worst Day Cycle, and our fear of success, avoid them altogether. Pursue more outside esteem through social media and status. Escalate our addictions, affairs, overeating, drinking, and drugging and stuff our emotions even more. As our health continues to decline, take more pills, belittle others, burn this book, send me and others like me hate mail, and tell me how wrong I am. Be angry. Do everything we can to avoid our trauma, fear, shame, and especially our denial. When we run out of pain, the answers will be waiting for us. No matter what we try to do, no matter how "bad" we are, the gift of our greatness that lies inside our darkness will never leave us. It is waiting for us on the other side.

If you are ready to begin exploring this, make a conscious choice to turn around and run headfirst into your trauma, fear, shame, and denial. Take time to explore them and become an expert on them. Your light, your greatness, your gift to your children and the world, and—most of all—yourself is in that darkness. There is no other way. Your journey to success depends on embracing your darkness.

Your Journey to Success Steps

1. Sit in critical thought and ask yourself, "What am I getting out of my current life situation? What is the payoff for the problems in it?"
2. If you are afraid to do something, go right at it immediately.
3. Outside of your original trauma, consider all of your resentments and hurts. Look at them until you can see how you set them up. Once you discover how you set them up, dig in and figure out what manipulations you used to create them.

Chapter Nine

The Power of Saying No

It all started with telling a server *no* for a glass of water. As my first marriage was ending, I began seeing a counselor. He noticed I didn't know how to say *no* and that I would impulsively say *yes* to things, so he gave me an assignment: "For the next week, I don't care what it is, I want you to first say *no* to any question. I want you to say *no* without even thinking about it. Then, take some time to think about it and if you decide it is something that works for you, after that evaluation go ahead and say *yes*." I left that appointment and went to dinner. The server approached and said, "Hi, would you like some water?" I began to shake and meakly stated, "No." I felt this chill run through my body and I was like… OMG, I had never done that. When she returned, I said, "You know what? I've thought about it, and I'd like some water." And I did that to her all night. The poor server was looking at me like "Jesus, are you ever going to say *yes*?" I left her a massive tip. But saying *no* changed my life; it changed my business. It taught me that *yes* can be the most manipulative, unloving, codependent thing we ever say to anyone.

Saying *No* at Work

When I was a contractor, one client wanted to install granite countertops. He asked, "Why don't you just give me your subcontractor's phone number and I'll deal with him directly?" I used to do that. I'd give the client the contact information and I'd lose my markup, which was essentially how I made my living. I did it because I wanted my clients to like me and give me a good referral. My thought process was, "If I do this and they see I'm giving them a deal, maybe…" That was bullshit. They never gave me the referral. Can you now see how saying *yes* to a request like that is a manipulation? By saying *yes*, I was covertly manipulating the other person to get something in return.

At that point, I was just a few days in on learning how to say *no*. My client was an older man, and talking to anyone in that age group felt to me like I was still talking to my father. My dad was always right, and I learned quickly I could never say no to him or argue with what he thought was right. It was my job to accept my dad's beliefs and thoughts, so that he could feel safe. You see, his dad was physically abusive and always right. While my dad never laid a hand on me, to deal with his own Worst Day Cycle, he adopted the "I am always right philosophy," too. I took a big deep breath and said, "You know, Jim, that's how I make my living. I would be more than happy to set this up for you and get this done, but I'm not willing to give you my subcontractor's information. Now if you would like to go hire someone else, you are more than welcome to do that and become your own general contractor. I will not stand in the way, but my contract says, if you hire your own people and that delays the job, there are costs involved with that. It's up to you." He looked at me and said, "No, that's fine; we'll just use your guy." That was the most powerful *no* I had ever said up to that point, because it was the first time I confronted my father's Worst Day Ever Cycle. And it all started by telling a server *no* for a glass of water.

Every client who I work with has to learn to say *no*, even the type-A personalities. It's a universal struggle. They tend to say *no* a lot but it is usually to control others and based on a fear of intimacy, of being known—that is, it's not a genuine *no*. They use *no* to create distance and false power. When I ask my more relaxed type-B clients to begin saying *no*, I often hear, "I'll feel guilty. I don't want to be mean." What they are really saying is something entirely different: "By saying *yes* to this, I can make the other person feel guilty." They are using that *yes* so they can then say, "Can you believe all I have done for Suzy and she never appreciates it? She owes me." How many times have we had that conversation with our friends? For me, it has been countless. We want to make the other person feel guilty to gain the victim power of the Worst Day Cycle, but we aren't aware of it yet. That's why we are saying *yes*. We are bartering and don't know the outcome. The Worst Day Cycle thrives on that powerlessness factor and the resulting self-victimizing false power.

Saying *No* in Personal Relationships

When I started dating the woman who would become my second wife, I told her, "Look, I have issues with people being late. It's my issue, not yours, and I have not reconciled it yet." My parents were quite often late (yes, being late as a parent is a form of trauma) and it made me feel inadequate, insecure, and unloved. I told her, "I have this thing, if we make plans and we decide to leave at a certain time, we leave at that time. That's what I have to do for me to keep me from resenting you. If we decide to meet somewhere at a particular time, I will be there at that time. If you are running late, if the resentment begins to build, to protect us both I might leave if that is what I need to do. You don't have to follow this rule, but I just want you to know that's what works for me." She told me she was almost always late.

Here's what happened: She was at my house one morning and we made plans to go to dinner that evening and leave at seven o'clock. About five minutes before seven, I looked in on her and saw there was no way that she was going to be even close to being ready on time. I didn't say a word. What I used to do was bitch and yell. Instead, at seven o'clock, without a word, I grabbed my keys, walked out the door, and got into my car. About ten minutes later, I got a text:

> Where did you go?

> I left. I'm on my way to dinner.

> **Why?**

> Why? Because I am going to dinner like we planned.

> **Well, why didn't you tell me?**

> But I did! I told you this morning when we made this plan that I was going to leave at seven o'clock. I guess you decided that didn't work for you and you would rather go at a different time. Or possibly you made other plans? I don't know. My hope is you still want to come and I will see you soon!

    She arrived about thirty minutes late, which is what she told me was her norm. To her credit, she didn't yell at me and accepted that I don't like to be late. I just did what works for me and, as you can see, so did she. That's a healthy *no*. I showed her authentically who I am, without controlling her and expecting her to meet my demands so I can feel safe inside. It's never the other person's job to make me feel good or fix my issues. It is my job to do it. In the end, we had a great night. She later thought about the experience and our relationship and realized the following: I never touch a car door or a chair, he helps me put my coat on, he drives (he doesn't drink so if I want to drink, I can do so and he will be the sober driver), and I don't have to spend gas money. With these considerations in mind, she determined she liked those things more than being late. Through our entire six-year marriage, she was late maybe four times. She adjusted her behavior not because I coerced her with a *yes* but because it worked for her. She found a new way to love herself.

    That's what saying *no* gives you. It shows a person who you are authentically and what works for you. This gives the other person a chance to ask, "Does that work for me or not?" If it doesn't, they move on. But if it does, they make adjustments. They want to spend time with this person because they do X, Y, and Z. Saying *yes*, on the other hand, creates resentment and a tally list. Here is how you can know if saying *yes* is a problem for you. If you have ever yelled at someone or silently raged because you have done so much for others and they don't appreciate it or recognize it, then you are saying *yes* to manipulate and control them. You are in your Worst Day Cycle and setting up your own self-victimization, and you are in denial about it.

Before we married, my wife was working at a local bar. I used to stop by every day and I noticed customers would buy her shots of liquor and she'd do the same at their table. I started getting pissed off and went back and thought about it. I came up with: There's nothing wrong with her doing shots. This is my issue. For whatever reason, she likes to do shots at work and flirt with men. I asked myself, "What can I control, and what works for me?" I thought about it. "Wait a minute," I told myself. "It's not okay for me to be dating someone who drinks at work and flirts with other men. It just doesn't work for me." Instead of yelling at her, telling her how inconsiderate she was to me, I made a decision. I would no longer stop by the bar and subject myself to seeing that. I also declared to myself and nobody else, "I'll give it ten days. If I don't see a change, then I am moving on." Again, it is my job to take care of me; it was not her responsibility.

After four days of me not stopping by, she texted me:

> Where have you been? Are you stopping by today?

> No.

> Why not?

> It doesn't work for me.

> It doesn't work for you?

> It just doesn't work for me.

> What does that mean? In what way?

> Well, I notice you drink and take shots with your customers and you flirt with them. It's not okay for me to sit there and see that, so I decided I wouldn't put myself through that anymore.

The point is, any problem in a relationship is my problem. That's what *no* teaches us. It's always about me. They are never the problem. If they hit me and I stay, then my mere presence is an implied *yes*. I am condoning it by staying. I either have to change me by accepting who they are or leave. It's not their responsibility to change for me. Our whole history of relationships—every movie, TV show, love song, and love story—has taught us the opposite. We have been fed a lie, told that they are supposed give up everything and change for us. That is a fantasy; it's not loving. It's manipulation and codependency, and it's why marriages don't work. But because no one knows this, eventually what you have is both sides saying, "I did this and you didn't do that." They fight over how they both gave up everything to manipulate the other person and get what they wanted. We aren't bad; we just don't know. It is just another way we exercise the Worst Day Cycle.

It was the day before my cutoff date with my now ex-wife; I never said a word about my deadline to her. We were out to dinner and she said, "You know, I've been thinking about something. I've decided I'm looking for a new job. I don't like that you don't come by, and I've also decided I'm going to limit myself to three drinks at a time from now on." Again, she looked at what was important to her on her own, without being manipulated and controlled, and she made an adjustment to her lifestyle. She did this because, in the end, it mattered more to her to do that. She didn't do it because I was demanding her to fix me or make me feel good inside. She did it because it made her feel good to be around me more.

The Reality of Saying *No*

My client Jay (the armoire guy) came in one day freaking out because he lost three clients that week. He said, "I'm on my cycle again, Kenny; I'm going back down. Everything is going wrong!" I asked him to tell me about his clients and he said, "Well, one guy was trying to get me to do stuff under the table, another wanted me to do this illegal stuff, and another kept trying to get me to do more stuff for free." I said, "Jay, say all of that to me again." He stared at me. I continued, "Remember who you were before you first hired me. You used *yes* to manipulate everyone and you overextended yourself. That's why your business failed and you lost everything. Here's what happened this week: there's still a remnant of that old you and that's why those three people hired you. They saw that and figured they could manipulate you. But now you say *no* and they fired you because they realized they can't manipulate you. The truth is you just broke your cycle. You broke it!"

They say you can't say *no* in business. In truth, that's the most valuable time to say *no*. In the past, Jay had never said *no* and he suffered some horrific financial consequences from this. Now, he's the leading agent in his real estate company and in the ten months since he started working with me, he has seen an 86 percent increase in his business. Agents are now looking to him as a mentor and guide. They want to know what he did to turn things around. He tells me they don't believe it came from working with a life coach like me, discovering his Worst Day Cycle, learning to say *no*, and facing his fear of success. That's not surprising when you consider how the brain works. If we don't know something, it sends us into fear and then quickly into denial to keep our self-victimization power alive. What Jay is explaining to others is unfamiliar to them. They were hoping he would attribute his success to a real estate class or a motivational book by Tony Robbins—something that they were already familiar with. That way their brain and body can keep firing the same emotional chemicals they have been firing for years. But, as a result, nothing changes. Despite all this knowledge about the power of saying *no*, I once again stopped saying *no* after I married my second wife.

The Day My Marriage Died

I know precisely the day my second marriage died. That's the day I stopped saying *no*. Until that point, I had been practicing a confrontation model my counselor taught me. Here's what that model included:
- share what you observed using "I" statements
- share what you deduced from that observation
- examine how you feel about what you are observing and fabricating
- if needed, ask the other person to consider making a change or ask for more information

Since we are using judgment about what we are observing and we can't get inside someone else's head, asking for information usually clears things up. If we do make a request, the final step is to celebrate their *no* because they are loving themselves authentically. This means they are loving you and not manipulating you by saying *yes*. One day while I was using this confrontation model with my wife, she blurted out, "Would you stop being so goddamned boundaried and just tell me what you really think and feel?"

Sitting at our kitchen table on a Sunday morning, I clutched my breath, tilted my gaze upward at the popcorn texture of the ceiling, and paused. Have you ever noticed how the mass of kernels sit suspended above you like a torrent of hailstones just waiting for the right conditions to explode? My response to her question would determine whether the two of us would be battered by that hail. As I stared at the hail trapped in the ceiling, I felt tremendous fear. I briefly contemplated not giving her what she asked for. I told myself, "Don't do it, Kenny; don't do it. She is just scared. You need to be strong for her, for the both of us." But I wanted her approval; I wanted her to like me; I wanted to please her. Wouldn't the loving thing be to give her what she wants? Shouldn't I say *yes*? So I did. I dropped the confrontation model and I gave her all of it.

For the next five years, I spewed it all without a filter. Everywhere we went, during every conversation and every activity, I released an avalanche of hail upon us both. Like a Buffalo winter, no matter how fast you shovel, the snow falls faster, covering whatever path you thought you had dug out. Our marriage died that day, but it took me several years to realize it. That one little *yes* turned into countless more. The accumulation of those *yeses* led me back to drinking after over twenty years of sobriety, an escalation in my sex addiction, and the decision to pursue a professional golfing career—something she wanted for me but that left me completely dependent upon her financially and emotionally. I was deep into my Worst Day Cycle again.

Another devastating consequence was the distance that slowly and imperceptibly began to creep into the marriage. The word *yes* creates that. About a year before our marriage ended, I attempted one last time to say *no* to her. We met with our counselor, the man who had originally taught me about boundaries and the value of saying *no* after my first marriage.

When we started dating, she began seeing his wife, also a counselor, who helped her learn the same skills. We married in part because we learned to speak the same language and share the same ideals. In short, my wife learned how to say *no* as well. In that meeting, I asked my wife to end an inappropriate relationship, an emotional affair she was having with her business partner. She replied, "No." Already knowing the power of *no*, I thought I would leave that instant, but then I couldn't. All of my little *yeses* had skewed my feelings and thinking so badly that I was now addicted to and imprisoned by the relationship and my Worst Day Cycle. I had no power and no safety; I could see no way out just like when I was a child. That is what saying *yes* did. It caused me to lose touch with who I am and, as I saw it, with my sanity as well.

The final straw came when I was lying in the sun enjoying a peaceful respite from the inner turmoil when out of nowhere a feeling and picture started to form in my brain and body. I saw and felt this tsunami coming toward me. You can't outrun something like that when you are in your Worst Day Cycle. It is too big, too powerful, so you just succumb. As I lay there in the crucifying Arizona sun, I was being enveloped by the coldness of the emotional wave that was washing over me. I felt myself carried back to my apartment. After three or four days of being dragged across the empty landscape inside my heart and mind, I called my wife. I hadn't seen her in two months. She was living and "pursuing business" in another state with the business partner she was having the emotional affair with. I told her she had to come home, that I didn't think she could do anything to help me but that I needed someone around or I was going to have to go into the psych ward. She came home.

A few months later, she made a choice that exploded her business partnership, thus ending the affair. For a brief time she turned back toward me. I knew it was only because she was afraid. But I couldn't verbally say *no* to her, so instead I used my sex addiction to communicate my *no*. When I am in my Worst Day Cycle, that is the best I can do. She said *no* to my behavior and we were formally separated shortly thereafter. The resulting withdrawal was severe and had me contemplating suicide. I had suffered tremendous physical and emotional trauma in my life but nothing compared to this. In retrospect, my choosing to drop my boundaries in the kitchen was manipulative and abusive to us both. My saying *yes* was an attempt to extract love from her. I wanted to make her like me, so I could feel better. That is my job, not hers. Conversely, her unwillingness to give up her emotional affair was incredibly loving. She told me exactly who she was and what was important to her. She was authentic to herself and to me. That is love! She was telling me that the marriage was no longer a priority in her life, that her business and this other person now were. I chose to ignore her honest rejection of the marriage and, in the process, further victimized us both. I say *no* a lot now. I have learned how loving that is to me and you.

When and How to Say *No*

We should say *no* if it goes against our morals and values or our needs and wants. Morals and values for most people rarely change, so that is pretty easy.

Needs are also constant because they are based on things necessary for our survival, like food, shelter, money, and relationships. Wants are more flexible and therefore a *no* today might be a *yes* tomorrow based on our wants or our emotional state in that moment.

Here are some simple guidelines. Say *no* if you believe at any point saying *yes* to a request will

- lead to resentment
- create a feeling of being owed something in return
- cause you to use it as a bartering chip for something someone isn't giving you

If we are feeling powerless and/or helpless in any area of our life, it is most likely because we are saying *yes* to things we want to say *no* to. If we think saying *no* will make us seem inconsiderate or if we feel guilty about it, then we most definitely need to say *no*. In these instances, saying *yes* is a sure indication of codependency and our Worst Day Cycle. There are times when saying *no* can be manipulative, too. That's when we are using it to control a person or to get back at them for not giving us a *yes* response to our request.

Your Journey to Success Steps

1. For the next week, when someone makes a request of you, say *no* first without even considering it. Then, take some time to see if you might use your *yes* against that person in the future. If you are certain you won't, then go ahead and say *yes* if you would like to.
2. Where do you feel powerless in your life? Where have you been saying *yes* to too many things? Where do you need to start saying *no*?
3. If you want to learn more about relationships and codependency, read Pia Mellody's *Facing Codependence*, *Facing Love Addiction*, and the *Intimacy Factor*.

Chapter Ten

Are You the Hostage or Hero in Your Career?

For many of us, the careers we choose are a direct reflection of the trauma we've experienced growing up. This does not necessarily mean we have chosen the wrong career. The reality is our current career choice is a gift; it's a passport into how our Worst Day Cycle began and how it is operating in our life. Whether we know it or not, we have chosen these careers in order to face our Worst Day Cycle.

Consider that nearly every Realtor I have met has had some sort of instability in their home while growing up. Whether they moved around a lot or they moved at an influential time in their childhood, whatever it was, something was unstable at home so they are now re-creating that instability through the process of buying and selling homes. In this industry, anything can happen. At the last minute, buyers may change their mind, financing might fall through, or the inspection may fail. To keep the deal together, Realtors are constantly bartering in this incredibly chaotic and fear-inducing process.

Engineers were told in some fashion that emotions were a problem, so they selected a career that is devoid of them. My father was an engineer who was physically abused as a child. Because of his trauma history, he shut himself off from his emotions to survive. He did not believe in self-help, therapy, or psychology. He loved being an engineer because it had structure and rules he could follow without emotion. The paradox was that my father was gifted emotionally. People who pursue careers in the military or become police officers or fire fighters were stripped of their power during childhood so they seek power-inducing uniforms and roles to fill that power vacuum. Someone who chooses a career in sales, especially fast-paced medical sales or car sales, was told directly or indirectly that they had no worth. Each and every day they have to prove their worth—they have no worth until they sell something.

Needing "insurance" is about a lack of safety. Something happened that left insurance professionals vulnerable, so now they are trying to "insure" that it doesn't happen again. Financial planners had some sort of event involving money. They are scared to death of having it or losing it. Those in helping professions, such as nurses, doctors, or massage therapists, were made to take care of others in some fashion so now they do it for a living.

My Career Choices and the Worst Day Cycle

My older brother and I fought for power growing up. We both wanted to be the leader in the household. The problem was he was a lot bigger than me, so he could literally hold me by my head and just laugh at me as I swatted away at thin air. I also felt that I had no voice because whenever I opened my mouth, I would be ridiculed by my family. Unlike my other family members, I have always seen and felt things from an emotional perspective. Due to my father's childhood trauma, he was an angry man who was distant and always needed to be right. I learned to stuff my anger because only he could express it or be right. It became my job to keep my mom sober, to listen to both of my parents' feelings, and therefore to take care of them.

Although my dad didn't pay a lot of attention to me, he expected me to listen to his angry tirades. He would argue with the TV whether it had something to do with politics or football. His opinions needed to be heard, as this was his opportunity to expel the emotions he was not allowed to express as a kid. I felt the only way I could get his attention was by listening to him. For years I thought hockey and golf were my true passions. Looking back, these sports allowed me to release my hidden anger; plus my dad would attend every hockey game I played and cheer me on. He was proud of my ability and that made me feel loved by him.

My first career was a hockey goalie. My dad was not pleased about my position choice, because goalie equipment is expensive. So the deal was that I, an eight-year-old kid, had to carry my hockey equipment bag to daily practice at the rink, which was eight blocks away. If I could carry the bag that was essentially the same size as me, I could play. Looking back, it was another backhanded way I could get my power back. It was like, "I can't get your attention, Dad, so watch me do this." I gravitated toward being a goalie for several reasons. For starters, when we played street hockey, my brother demanded I get in the net. I realized quickly that if I stopped the puck from going into the net, it would piss him off. I liked that. It was the one and only place I could, in a sense, beat him up. I learned to withstand slap shots that riddled my body with bruises to get power over my brother. It was pure self-victimization. Goalies are like kickers in football. Nobody talks to them. It's almost like they are not human. Think about it: who would want to stand in front of a puck coming at you at speeds up to 100 mph? Goalies must be weird. I always felt my family also thought I was weird, so I relived that feeling by becoming a goalie. On the team, no one talks to the goalie and you don't sit on the bench with your teammates. You stand alone throughout the whole game on an island. This position allowed me to relive the chemical cocktail of isolation. Finally, who is to blame when a goal is scored? Me. Who can I then yell at? Me. I became a goalie so that I could stand out there all alone and berate myself. I could dump the anger that I was never allowed to express as a kid.

I did not know that I was reliving my worst day by retraumatizing myself, so I pursued more hockey opportunities after high school. At times, while playing junior hockey in Canada or when I was trying to get a pro tryout, I would sleep in locker rooms and in parks with all of my equipment and suitcases. I would hitchhike from town to town, sometimes standing on a corner for as long as fourteen hours. I didn't stay in hotels because I didn't have money for that, and my dad did not want me being dependent on him.

While I was practicing with the Vancouver Canucks, one of the players knew I was sleeping in parks so he invited me to his house for dinner and to sleep inside. My emotional need to relive the trauma cycle kept me from accepting his offer. I could not say *yes*. I remember thinking, "What a great story this will be when I make it into the big time." I had turned my self-victimization into self-power. I was doing it to myself so I could spin it into something to manipulate others.

Another example came as the season ended when I was playing in the minor leagues. I remember sitting on the plane flying back home looking out the window and it hit me. I heard, "You're going to make it; you're that good. Whatever you do, don't get messed up with a woman this summer." Here's another great reason why thoughts don't drive behavior. Three weeks later, I became engaged to a girl I had been friends with for about a year. Four months later, I went to training camp. The two other goalies were under contract while I was a free agent. One of those goalies ended up playing six years in the NHL and the other had just come off winning the Olympic Gold Medal and played fourteen years in the NHL. The coach pulled me aside and said, "Kenny, you're the best goalie we have in camp but you know how it goes; these two are under contract. I wish I could keep you but we're going to have to let you go." I had other offers to continue playing, but my fiancée told me, "I don't think we will make it if you keep playing." She didn't tell me *not* to play, but my abandonment fears from my Worst Day Cycle got the best of me. That was the end of my hockey career.

I then spent the next ten years as a general contractor and custom furniture maker. My first wife thought it would be a good career fit for me. I switched from trying to please my dad with hockey to trying to please her. I was a sole proprietor, so most of the time I had the business I was once again alone. Let me make this clear, she did nothing wrong; I did this all to myself. I was choosing people and setting situations up to victimize myself and play the victim so I could point the finger at them. None of us were bad people in these dynamics; we just didn't have the information to know what we were doing to ourselves. In my second marriage, my wife kept talking about how she wanted me to give golf another try as a career. I had been a pretty good player in high school and still was. After a few years of her efforts to persuade me, I gave it a shot. What it did was leave me completely dependent upon her emotionally and financially. Plus, it was a solitary pursuit that filled me with anger and self-hatred. When I hit a bad shot, I was to blame.

Reconciling Your Trauma

Here's something important to note: I am by no means suggesting that you quit your job because you are traumatizing yourself. That's not the point at all. However, go ahead and ask yourself if your career is keeping you in the Worst Day Cycle. And if so, determine if there is a way out. Here's the good news: even if it is keeping you in your Worst Day Cycle, there's a gift in there. It can give you valuable insights into how you are reliving that cycle. It can open doors to answers you haven't been willing or able to find. Each time we repeat our trauma, we peel back another layer that reveals how we are trying to gain the power back that we lost as a kid and we gain a better understanding of the original trauma. Today, I'm a coach, professional speaker, and author. I'm once again totally repeating my trauma, but in this career, I'm also reconciling it. For the first time in my life, I have selected my current career for myself. I didn't get to speak as a kid. I always felt that my thoughts and belief systems were shunned by my father and family. Now people come to me as an expert. I stand on a stage—separated, still alone—but at least I am being heard. I'm reliving the same dynamic as I sit there and listen to my clients in my office, just like I sat and listened to my dad and mom. While in one sense nothing has changed, the difference is people actually pay to hear my thoughts and beliefs. I've reconciled it.

You may think this doesn't apply to you and your career choice, but remember how denial works. We have to keep the self-concept we were given to keep our attachment to the parent who sent the message. If we step past the message they sent us about ourselves, then we are in essence breaking our bond with them. When it comes to procrastination, look at who either directly or indirectly said you weren't good enough or you weren't worthy. Maybe it was a parent or teacher asking, "Why are you so messy all the time? You'll never get anywhere if you keep that up." How did you feel at that moment when you heard you weren't good enough? That's the trauma that generates the Worst Day Cycle. This is what happened to my client David.

David came to see me because he felt he wasn't doing enough in his professional life. Although he owns his own mobile tire-changing service, he felt capable of more. He said, "I want to do something life changing. I want to make a bigger impact. I want to change people's lives." For the first couple of sessions, we discussed his lack of motivation and the procrastination that prevented him from pursuing bigger things. His father was an alcoholic, never recognized David's accomplishments, and believed his children would never move out of the extreme poverty they lived in. His father even asked David, "Why would people hire you to do that?" Because of his own trauma, his father could not accept his son moving beyond what he had accomplished. I helped David to see how his father's drinking and beliefs were directly affecting him, causing him to not pursue bigger opportunities.

David arrived for his appointment one day upset. He said, "I'm just not doing anything with my life. I'm a failure. All I do is change tires. I don't do anything of value." Then he told me two stories. One was about a client whose trailer got a flat as they were headed out of town for a family reunion. They couldn't find a replacement tire anywhere, but David had one for them. This trip was very important to them. They were just gushing about him and his ability to get them on the road again. He told me how they thanked him and hugged him for having this type of mobile tire-changing service. David shared that he was angry at them for thinking what he did mattered. Then David shared a second story.

He received a phone call from a grandmother who had a special tire on her car that had been flat for a month because nobody had the specific wrench needed to change it. David had the right wrench. The woman was caring for her granddaughter. After David changed the tire, he didn't understand why this woman was so incredibly grateful to him. I could see why but David couldn't. After the tire was changed, the granddaughter asked, "Does this mean I don't have to walk to school anymore? Does this mean we can go for ice cream now?" The grandmother responded with, "Yes, yes it does."

I asked David if he could imagine why they were so thankful. I said, "David, these people have been prisoners inside their home. They haven't been able to live life because they haven't had use of this car, and now this six-year-old granddaughter doesn't have to walk to school and can go out and have ice cream with her grandma. David, you don't change tires. You change people's lives." He just sat there dumbfounded. Because of the shame and pain he felt from his upbringing, he couldn't recognize that he was already changing people's lives. I told him what a wonderful tagline it would be for his business, "I don't change tires, I change lives." When he finished sharing his stories, I said, "Do you remember what you told me about your father? How do your feelings and these stories relate?" With these questions, it became clear to him. He was already accomplishing what he wanted—he was doing something life changing. He was also reconciling his Worst Day Cycle but was completely unaware of it. This was a clear example of someone holding onto his father's belief system so he wouldn't have to sever the only emotional tie he had to him.

Now that we know why we choose the careers we do, look at your career choices past and present. Acknowledge the gift you have been given to look at your worst day and transform it into the best day.

> ### Your Journey to Success Steps
> 1. What kinds of emotions does your career evoke? How do those emotions tie into your worst day? Are they harmful or helpful?
> 2. What emotional condition is your career satisfying? By asking this, you will instantly know the basic framework of where your trauma cycle started and why you are in this career.

Chapter Eleven

The "Let It Come" Approach

Note: The following is an email I sent to my counselor in March 2015:

I am really struggling today. I have walking pneumonia and I feel depressed and defeated. These feelings have been prevalent for the last few years and in the past twelve to eighteen months they have become debilitating. Imagine waking in the morning, walking into the kitchen, pouring gas all over you, and lighting yourself on fire. The rest of the day, you smell it, feel it, and promise yourself that you will do whatever it takes to not do it again. But you wake up the next day and without the slightest fight, you go into the kitchen and light yourself on fire again.

I have this compulsion to live in pain. I repeatedly choose a life that brings me pain. I tried watching the improv comedy television show Whose Line Is it Anyway? the other day. I couldn't keep watching it. I kept flipping back, trying to watch it, but it made me so uncomfortable. It made me remember that when I would go to comedy clubs I rarely laughed. That's because it is not okay for me to be happy. It is uncomfortable and wrong and makes me afraid. Yes, I am afraid to be happy. Happiness to me means that something bad will happen and that pain is on its way. I have a ton of anger from my choices and things out of my control that have happened to me, but I can't feel the anger in my body or heart. I know it is there but I have no connection to it. I realize anger and my compulsion to fail or feel less than drive my acting out, my addictions. I don't know how to stop these feelings and choices. I am aware of the process.

I tell others to go to meetings, make phone calls, and do affirmations, but I can't do them. I am completely powerless to stop my fears, thoughts, and actions. As author Eckhart Tolle says in his book, The Power of Now, we are constantly caught up in the "story" of our life instead of the "now." He mentions that in moments like this, the key is to surrender to the suffering, that pain like this is a blessing because it is so bad, you become willing to surrender. I feel that way. I am exhausted from all the suffering I have endured and chosen. This life is not one I want to live anymore. I am so unhappy all day, every day. I see and hear people saying, "Just do this. Don't do that." But it doesn't work that way for me. I can't stop what goes on in my thoughts. I pray, I meditate, I breathe, I go to Twelve Step meetings, make phone calls… but I am always at this point.

I can't run my life anymore. I'm a failure at it. I have so much proof of that. I don't want to die. I don't want that for the people around me but I don't see this pain, this continual process of pain I either choose or that happens to me, ending. I have a stretch of doing "the right things" and feeling a shade above misery, but I always at some point fail in some way and end up back here. I can't stop the cycle and I can't live with this cycle anymore. I may be here in form but I am dead inside and my sense of hope recedes with each failure or the return of this pain. I have always had an insane ability to withstand pain both physically and emotionally. I have been able to survive (not overcome) many painful things. I am at a point where I no lon-

ger have that resolve. I am worn out and don't feel the strength to fight like I used to. I am surrendering to the pain in a way. However, all that is behind that surrender is emptiness. I don't know what to do, where to go, or how to stop this cycle I choose.

Let Go of Control and Let It Come

In that email I hadn't fully put the pieces of the Worst Day Cycle together yet, but you can see them riddled throughout the email. I am screaming at myself to let go of the false self that was created to survive my original traumas. I am aware of my self-abuse as I talk about how I bounce between worlds. I am trying to find the real me, but I am at war with myself. I chose to include this email because I feel it is probably something almost everyone can identify with. I see in people's faces this internal hell on a daily basis. I wanted to bring hope from a place of feeling no hope. I had no idea that I was inches away from my greatness and my light—all I could see was darkness and death.

When I wrote that email, I was in the midst of my second divorce and contemplating suicide. My inability to stop "lighting myself on fire" each morning was becoming too much. I wanted out. The problem was that I knew too much. As I considered how I would explain all of this in a suicide note to my kids, I just kept saying, "That's bullshit, that's manipulative." I knew too much psychology to be able to outthink myself. That left me only one choice.

Ever since I found my mom passed out in the bathroom, I had been on hyper alert, trying to outthink, outmaneuver, and control everything and everyone I came in contact with. I did this to try to keep myself safe, to make sure I never experienced that moment again. I hadn't discovered it at the time, but that is what the shame portion of the cycle does to us. We feel so powerless that we attempt to control everything and all of that control becomes self-victimizing. Without being aware of it, we kill ourselves with our own control. It was clear to me as I wrote that email that all of my efforts weren't working. I had only one option left. I was going to have to wake up the next morning and *not* know what was going to happen and stop trying to figure it out. It was the only thing I hadn't tried.

As I walked to my bedroom that night, I knew the life I had been living was about to end. I was going to go to bed as one person and in the morning that person would be long gone, much like the person that left me forty years earlier when I found my mom. I awoke the next morning and made my way to the edge of the kitchen. I stood there, tears starting to form, and I heard myself ask, "What do I do now?" For the first time, there was no flurry of options, answers, or incessant talk. My mind was quiet. Eventually I heard, "Go sit on the couch." This process continued. My mind was quiet and guidance or a direction was coming to me. I was letting life come to me. I was no longer being a grinder and thinking things to death, obsessing over them, trying to control them, or being afraid of things not working out. I had learned how to "let it come."

This new "let it come" philosophy or approach to living began to take hold. Growing up, I was not allowed to be angry. It was not okay for me to experience joy or anger, so I selected two sports where I could expel my anger. I didn't play those sports because I loved them. I played them so I could get angry with myself. For me, going out to play golf is now self-abuse. It's pure self-hatred. That's why I don't play anymore. Each time I swung the club, I would trigger that pain of the trauma I was carrying. I was still attempting to play golf after my "let it come" epiphany. A few days later, I went to the driving range to hit some balls and practice. With each ball I was becoming more pissed off and enraged. I finally stopped myself and asked, "What is going on?" Then it came to me. I made a commitment to myself that day: I decided to let go of control and that I was not going to hurt myself anymore. I left after hitting just a few balls. The next morning, I woke up and as I considered going to the driving range, I asked myself, "How are you feeling?" I wasn't feeling it and I was still pretty upset, so I didn't go. The next day I went to the driving range and an hour into it, I once again became ticked off so I left. I told myself, "I will not let myself be this angry." It took about a week or so before I went back. But within thirty minutes of arriving at the golf course, I was so filled with rage and frustration, I stopped. I said, "That's it. I'm done with golf. I am not going to do this to myself anymore. I will not hate myself like this." I put the clubs in the bag and have only touched them three times since then. I refuse to hurt myself anymore that way.

Try Something Different

Then came the next layer of learning how to let it come. I was still unsure what I was going to do for full-time work, so I was temporarily driving for Uber. In the middle of the day, I dropped somebody off. I sat there for a few minutes and realized I wasn't getting another rider. Typically, I would drive around in circles looking for another fare, always sure that if I could get to the right part of town, I could pick somebody up. I was always trying to control the situation.

This would inevitably bring frustration and self-hatred. I knew I had to try something different. I pulled into a hotel parking lot and parked. That's when I started to rage. I was pissed off and the tears were streaming down my face. I desperately wanted to make it happen by driving around. I had to get control of the situation. As I raged, this new voice that had shown up that first morning kept saying, "No, Kenny, you have to sit here; you have to let it come. That controlling is killing you. You can't go back to that pain." It took about thirty minutes before I finally started to calm down. I began to feel peace. I realized I didn't have to figure everything out and be in control. For me, control was a by-product of my parents, both finding my mom that day in the bathroom and trying to get my dad to like me. In the confines of my car that day, I was really able to let all of that go. That's when I heard the ding on my phone. I got my next rider. I put the car into gear and realized this is true fate. It will come to you when you stop chasing it. And that's what I do to this very day. I don't work like I used to. I don't grind. I don't "just do it." I don't think things to death or obsess, control, or fear things won't work out.

I took this same approach to discovering what my next career would be. I had no idea what I would do for a living beyond being an Uber driver. Every time I found myself obsessing about what I should do, I would smile and remind myself, "Just let it come, Kenny; just let it come." One day I flipped on the television and the show *Selling New York* was on and Louis, this over-the-top personality, was explaining how incredibly stressed out and overwhelmed he was with life. Very dramatically, he stated, "So, I called my life coach." I broke out laughing. I knew instantly, with all of the years of reading and working on my own recovery and how much I had enjoyed running support groups in the past, that this was the career for me. Thanks to Louis, in a flash I saw my whole life story and how every career and choice up to that moment had been on-the-job training as a coach. I have done and been through so much that I had not only the technical knowledge but the life experience to match it. I had gotten out of the way and it had come to me once again.

What Happens When You Let It Come

I have these phases where I lose nearly all of my clients. It is a natural part of the growth process. But the first time it happened, I began to panic and started to drop into fear and obsess about how I could fix it. I heard that now familiar voice, "Kenny, you are doing it again. Just let it come." When I got quiet, I heard, "You need to get smarter." I spent the next three weeks lying by the pool with no money coming in while living off credit cards. But I knew it was the right decision. Those three weeks and the research I did during that time provided me with the science of how the Worst Day Cycle works. It was no longer just a theory I had based on my intuition and experience. Now I could prove its validity and give my clients the tools they needed to overcome it.

As I began to think about the content of this chapter, I had no idea how to start it. The old Kenny would sit as his desk and grind it out. Instead, I went to the pool and lay in the sun. I got quiet and focused on what I could hear. I listened to the birds chirping, the wind glancing off of the tree leaves, my own breath. Slowly I started to calm down and began nodding off. As I learned how to let it come, one of the things I did was listen to guided meditation. Being able to focus on someone else's voice instead of the one in my head helped quiet the voices inside me. I found that there is a meditative state that comes just before sleep. Albert Einstein used to access it every day after lunch. He would sit in a chair with an apple in his hand. If he dropped the apple, it would startle him enough so he wouldn't sleep but it didn't completely wake him. While in this state, all extraneous thought goes away and you get pure clarity. As I approach sleep, I get flooded with insight, so now I keep my phone right next to me and I just "puke" my thoughts right into my phone for later retrieval.

I can now do the same thing when I go to the gym. I focus on what my body feels like and on my breath as I exercise. I don't count any of the repetitions. I have no idea how many reps I ever do. I keep my gaze focused straight ahead. If it starts to bounce around, that lets me know I'm in fear so I focus on what I can hear and feel to calm my amygdala down. Invariably, when I finish, solutions come to me regarding some area of my life. I don't pick the topic or "try" to figure something out. I now understand that answers will come to me when I don't force them. All of these other control-type idiosyncrasies that I once had are now gone. For instance, I had a habit of counting everything. I learned to do that when my dad would yell at me. I would stand there and look past him and find something behind him to count, like the stripes in the wallpaper. Sometimes I would look at license plates and do math with the numbers. Whatever I could find, I would count it. If I rolled my tongue in my mouth on one side to get a piece of food out, I had to do the other side. Everything in my life had to be equal. I couldn't just touch one side—I had to touch both. I see this all the time with clients; we all have these little things we do to try to control our fear, shame, and denial.

The "let it come" philosophy takes time and patience. How much time depends on each person and situation. When I became aware of all the ways my feelings, thoughts, and actions were contributing to my own demise, it freed me from obsessing over the power and control I was victimizing myself with. In my case, this didn't happen until I had inflicted so much pain upon myself that it broke me. As you read in my email, I could not stop "lighting myself on fire." My hope is that you will choose not to inflict that much pain on yourself. However, you may need to. Due to the centuries of bias against dealing with our emotions, we usually only address pain when it becomes tremendous. It doesn't have to be that way. We can make it okay to admit our imperfections. By doing so, we can create a whole new way to live that causes much less pain to ourselves and others and ultimately gets us all living in our best day cycle.

Your Journey to Success Steps

1. Read *The Power of Now* by Eckhart Tolle.
2. Download the free meditation app, Insight Timer. Try to meditate each day, even if it is just for five minutes.
3. Learn to focus on listening to your breath. Your brain stops thinking while you do this.

Chapter Twelve

The Beginning of a New Journey

There is a reward that comes from becoming educated and facing our worst day ever. For me, it came about shortly before my dad's death. The actual process started almost thirty years earlier when I first got sober from alcohol in my early twenties. At that time, I was away at college and I carefully crafted him a letter. I told him how I just wanted to know him. I wanted to know what he liked, what he didn't like, and what his dreams were as a kid. I wrote, "I just want to be your friend." You see, my father had been physically beaten as a kid. While he never hit my siblings or me, he was filled with rage. He had no information on how to deal with his feelings. I became someone he could control with that anger in his own attempt to overcome his worst day ever.

My parents had four kids by the time they were twenty-one and twenty-three. They were essentially children raising children. Fresh from their own traumatic childhoods, they became parents. They did the best they could but because of the physical abuse he endured as a child, my dad couldn't connect or get close with us early on. He was also overwhelmed with the responsibilities of raising four children, getting his degree, and beginning his career as an engineer. Even without his history of abuse, our parents took on a monumental task.

About a month or so after I wrote that letter, about thirty years ago, I came home from college. One day about a week later, my dad came up from the basement while I was in the kitchen and said to me, "Kenny, I got your letter and you just need to get over that." I was devastated. I had reached out to my father and once again he told me I was bad and wrong for wanting to get to know him. I wanted him to love me in the way I needed to be loved. What I heard was, "You're the problem, Kenny."

Fast forward to September 2017. I am now a life coach building my business as a public speaker. Because of my dad's abuse as a child, he learned to shut down his emotions to protect himself. He never thought psychology or therapy was of any value. What is interesting is that my dad would be the first one to tell you how he had tremendous personality problems when he was younger. He couldn't relate to people and he would alienate them. He even got fired from a prominent job because of his personality struggles.

But who my dad was when he died was completely different from who he was when we were children. My dad would regularly sit in critical thought. He was a keen observer of people. He would notice that when he said or did certain things, people would reject him. He noticed that people who had lots of friends acted and behaved differently than he did. We had long discussions about his struggles when he finally opened up to me before he died. As I sat listening, I discovered a man I had never known before. This man who never studied psychology or human development had an instinct. Throughout my life, my family thought I was most like my mother and my gifts of feeling and reading people came from her. While it is true she was gifted and I got my ability to feel others' pain and see evil from her, during the six months or so when we knew my dad was dying, I discovered that it was my dad who was the most gifted. I was so much more like him than I ever knew. In those discussions with my dad, I learned he had the ability to see goodness and greatness in others; he just didn't know it.

With that understanding as a backdrop, I kept my conversations about the type of work I do very superficial. He didn't want to go near emotional topics. One day when I called him, he asked me about work. I gave him the same generic response about getting new clients and preparing for some speeches. Out of the blue, he said, "Kenny, what you're doing is wrong. You're hurting people. You need to stop. Do you think I wanted to give myself cancer?" At that point, I realized he must have seen my YouTube video where I discussed how our emotions make us sick and how the most effective cancer treatment is emotional work. As author Louise Hay points out, it's usually some sort of deep hurt, a deep self-resentment, and/or someone who's been hiding and carrying a secret.

When we have an autoimmune disease, one body system is trying to kill another. This is when our body turns on itself. Isn't that how we all feel when we have been deeply hurt, we resent someone, or we keep a secret? I remember at one stage in my father's cancer treatment, his body was covered in unexplained welts and bruises. The doctors had no clue where they came from, though it was suspected to be an allergic reaction. I knew right away what those welts and bruises were all about. They were a visual manifestation of the beatings my father took as a child coming to the surface. All of that stored anger, hurt, resentment, and pain was trying to come out.

When my dad told me I was hurting other people through my work, I immediately became defensive and angry. "Whoa dad, I never said that and you can't do this to me, not this time," I said. "Every time I start to succeed, you try and take it from me. I won't let you do it this time." You see, throughout my life my dad would criticize me whenever I started to find success and tell me I was doing it wrong. Because of how denial works and my not wanting to let go of the only way I could stay connected to him, I would withdraw from whatever I was doing.

Now my dad calmly replied, "Kenny, your response tells me something." Instantly, I flashed through the Worst Day Cycle. He was right. I was in anger, which is a mask for fear of rejection, inadequacy, or powerlessness. I was feeling all of those in that moment. Being aware of this, I said, "Dad, you're right. I am angry because I'm scared to death. For the first time in my life, I am going to succeed. I am stepping into my greatness and it scares the hell out of me. I've never been down this road and I don't know what to do about it. But whenever I've been here, you have always tried to take it from me. Well, not this time. I won't carry it for you anymore. Dad, these are your thoughts, your feelings, and your issues. I will not fix them for you anymore. You're going to have to reconcile them on your own. It is no longer my job."

My dad had just helped me. I had confronted a long-standing fear, a neural pathway that had been firing for years. I finally dealt with *that* feeling that kept coming up. By doing so, I addressed the trauma, fear, self-victimizing shame, and denial. For most of us, the fear around confronting *that* feeling is too much, so we continue to repeat what we have always done.

In that phone conversation with my dad, I confronted my fear of success. I realized that the reason my dad would always try to sabotage my life and belittle me was because I was the part of himself he couldn't acknowledge. My dad was gifted emotionally but he had shut himself off from his emotions. When he saw me, he saw himself. My dad did not hate me or try to sabotage me. It had nothing to do with me. Although my dad was beating me down, he was really beating himself down.

Now that I know how denial works, I can see that truth. When we are in denial, we project and judge those who are like us because we can't see us. I reminded my dad of a part of him he was never taught how to access, a part he had to shut down to survive his trauma. My heart broke for him because, as brilliant as he was, he just didn't have this information. The denial he was taught—that we all have been taught—is what I believe killed him. Knowing this, I can forgive us both.

As the conversation ended, I said, "Dad, I love you. You're always teaching me something." He replied, "Kenny, I don't want to teach you anything. I just want to be your friend." When I hung up the phone, I broke down in tears. I recalled the letter from thirty years earlier when I asked him to be my friend. I realized that letter was all about me—I was trying to extract something from him that he could not give at that time. I wanted him to love me in the way that I needed. It was purely selfish. I was too young and didn't have the tools that I have now to love and accept my dad for who he was and the ways he was capable of loving me. I wanted to change him and make him something he didn't know how to be. In that phone conversation, I loved him unconditionally. I did that by no longer changing who I was in an attempt to steal his affection. I also told him authentically who I was and most importantly I loved him dearly when I told him *no*. I essentially told him, "I will no longer sacrifice who I am to please you. I will not carry your trauma anymore." You see, that's the value of telling somebody *no*. In that conversation, I became safe enough for my dad to drop his walls and ask me to be his friend. All of the things I did—trying to play hockey, trying to play golf, trying to listen to him and be a support to him—none of those gave him the love he was searching for, because I did them to try to manipulate him to love me. When we say *yes* to things to try to get people to like us, we are trying to steal love from them.

All of my efforts to get my dad to love me were self-centered. I finally got what I needed when I stepped into my success and claimed it. I did that by facing my Worst Day Cycle and learning how to love and forgive myself for how manipulative that cycle taught me to be. In that moment, I didn't need my dad to be my friend or be anything for me, because I had learned how to do it for myself. That's what happens in this process. We no longer need it from other people because when we have seen all of us, especially the dark parts we are in denial about, we generate it inside ourselves. And, when we do, other people come alongside us and love us, too. Even better, they want to be our friend. During this phone conversation with my father, I was able to see me and my own denial. And just like that, I was set free from my worst day ever. So here I sit having confronted my cycle as much as I know how. My ending the cycle with my father was the biggest aspect of that. These are words, thoughts, and beliefs that differ from his. For the first time, they are mine and writing this book is the next step. I have to use the tools to fight off that Worst Day Cycle feeling that comes up, so I can step into this. It scares me. I am embarking on my best day cycle, attempting to step into my inherent greatness, the greatness I believe we all have. I have no emotional marker for how to handle any of this, nothing to draw from, nothing that is comfortable. What I do have is me—the clearest understanding of who I am and the deepest level of personal acceptance I have known. I actually like myself now. I am not a perfect parent, friend, coach, brother, or person, but I no longer have to be. I have forgiven myself. Accepting my darkness gave me that ability.

In the following chapter, you will find the tools and process I have used personally and shared with my clients. I have culled information from some great people and am attempting to add to their wisdom and greatness. If I can ever be of help in any way, reach out to me directly or follow me on these platforms.

www.CoachKennyWeiss.com
Facebook: Kenny Weiss
LinkedIn: Kenny Weiss
YouTube: Kenny Weiss
Instagram: CoachKennyWeiss

Appendix

Your Journey to Success Toolkit

You can use certain activities to transform your worst day into your best day. Each activity applies to each phase of the Worst Day Cycle—trauma, fear, shame, and denial. Use a journal, notebook, or your computer to record your answers. You will find bonus activities on my website www.kennyweiss.com.

Activity 1: Dealing with Your Trauma on Your Journey to Success

Directions: There are certain activities you can do to transform your worst day into your best day. Dealing with your feelings is crucial in getting over your trauma in the Worst Day Cycle. This exercise will help you become more aware of what feelings are triggering the moods and choices you make.

Feelings

1. Do an Internet search for "feelings list."
2. There are many "feelings lists" on the Internet so take the time to choose one that appeals to you.
3. Print out the list and keep track of your feelings for an entire week by placing check marks next to the specific feeling so you know how often you are experiencing it.

4. Also note what was going on that triggered these specific feelings.

Once you have identified the recurring feelings, ask: "When was the first time I felt this?"

This is crucial. Don't judge your answer or view it as wrong. Whatever the first memory is, investigate it. It might be something from your adult life or when you were a child. People often discount that original answer and think, "Well, it wasn't that big of a deal." You might even believe that the memory that shows up isn't accurate. Don't do that. Whatever pops up, look at it and learn about it. You are beginning to unlock the trauma that you have denied or minimized.

As you do this, you are also unlocking the feelings inside your body. As you recall, that is where we store memories. Our bodies are a window into different traumas. Over time our brain and body will begin releasing those memories and we will begin to remember all the things we denied and repressed. This is the starting point to getting out of our worst day. It's time to begin to learn what is triggering our feelings. Write down some of those memories.

No feeling is bad. When we experience "bad" feelings, we instantly don't like them and have a tendency to medicate them away in many different ways. Avoiding uncomfortable feelings is primarily what keeps us in the Worst Day Cycle. Feelings are there to communicate what is going on in our life. If I feel depressed, that means I am doing something to create that feeling. It can also mean I am having a sad day. Feeling sad is wonderful; there is nothing wrong with it. I have learned to enjoy my "off" days. They bring color and insight into my life. For many people, this may be the first time they are even aware they are experiencing feelings. They have kept themselves so busy and therefore so numb that they have completely shut themselves off. They will have to begin the thawing-out process. This feelings exercise is a great start.

Activity 2: Using Affirmations to Build Self-Esteem

Directions: Affirmations are a great way to build self-esteem. I have two simple ways to build that self-esteem twice a day—in the morning and evening.

Note: Self-esteem is self-generated. Sadly, our culture promotes what is called other esteem. We attempt to derive our esteem from outside sources. This rarely works. In the U.S., we equate success with our looks, vehicles, homes, careers, zip codes, social media profiles, and popularity. We judge others and ourselves based on how much or how little of these things we have. Because of that, we generally wake up each day concerned that we don't have enough of these outside things, and so we feel less than and our self-talk matches that feeling. To counteract that pattern, we need to begin acknowledging who we really are.

1. Morning affirmations

Begin each morning with three affirmations. Write down three things you like about yourself. When beginning, do not just think them. Instead, say them out loud and then write them down.

An actual chemical reaction occurs when we write something down. That is why journaling is so popular and recommended by therapists. This is how we create that new neural pathway of our best day.

Here's an example of a typical morning for me. My morning routine consists of getting out of bed and, for whatever reason, I say, "I love my feet." Silly, I know, but it's how I feel. I then go over to my mirror, look myself right in the eye, and say, "I love you, Kenny."

Go to a mirror and say, "I love you, _____."

It is not about what you say; it is about creating and firing the feeling of things you like about yourself. If those kind words don't really describe how you feel about yourself, start with a question like, "What if I did like/love myself? What would that feel like?"

Now look in the mirror and ask, "What if I did love myself? What would that feel like?"

Just asking that question will flip a switch. Start sitting in that feeling and say, "Now that I know what it feels like to love myself, I am willing to allow myself to feel that." Just being willing to like/love any part of yourself is a big step to counteracting that worst day chemical.

2. Evening accomplishments

At the end of each day, write down three things you accomplished. By doing so, you will go to bed firing those best-day chemicals, which will shift your mood the following morning. Since most of us have no memory of our best day, the other great benefit of this is we now have good memories to draw upon. The importance of this exercise is to change our brain. It naturally remembers three negatives. I want to teach our brains to do the opposite. Additionally, when a bad day comes, you can always look back at these lists to help you get out of the Worst Day Cycle and combat it with these best day feelings.

Activity 3: Mirror Work

Directions: Mirror work is one of the most powerful tools on our journey to success. I first learned about mirror work from author Louise Hay. I started by looking in the mirror and stating out loud, "I love myself." Yes, it felt awkward but I made a point of saying it as often as possible. Just saying the words had little effect on me. Besides the positive self-talk, I needed positive self-feelings to create maximum impact. Even though I really didn't feel like I loved myself, I kept asking, "What would it feel like if I did love myself?" As I brought up that feeling, I said the words, "I love myself." Things really started to take off at that point.

The mirror is an amazing tool. It will show you things that are hidden as it finds the truth in you. Sadly, most of us are terrified of this exercise. Feeling frightened by it or thinking it is somehow silly is a clear sign of how much we need to do it. Take any situation in your life where you want a different outcome or feeling. Go to the mirror and ask yourself, "What would it feel like if this situation were the way I wanted it?" Begin feeling that feeling. If you hesitate, say, "I am willing to allow this new perspective, outcome, and feeling in my life."

After about two weeks of saying, "I love myself," I was looking in the mirror when out of nowhere, from deep inside, I heard a voice saying, "What about Kenny?" I paused, considered it, and said, "I love you, Kenny." I was instantly confused, afraid, and shocked. I could have sworn I heard a different voice. I asked, "What just happened?" I said it again and there it was. I was certain it was someone else's voice now. I did it a third time and it hit me. I literally could not hear my voice. I knew it was me talking but the voice I heard was my mother's voice. I broke down crying. I realized why I could never accept or believe it when a woman said she loved me. You see, when my mom would drink she would constantly tell me how much she loved me; she even went so far as to ask me, "Kenny, if I want to drink, can you give me a hug so that I won't drink?" Of course it never worked, but that message was stuck—frozen deep in my subconscious. It took me about two more weeks before I could hear my own voice say, "I love you, Kenny." I never realized my mom's voice was a cemented neural pathway that played when someone said they loved me. When my brain received new sensory feedback via the mirror, it began the process of shifting into a new belief.

When we go to the mirror with new feelings and the words to match them, our brain reorients itself. We can now become our best day.

Activity 4: Self-Care

Do you struggle with self-care? Most of us do. There are three questions you can ask and answer to propel you into self-care mode. Are you ready? See my website, www.coachkennyweiss.com, to download the worksheet.

Activity 5: Fear Work

Directions: The key to fear work is to calm our brain so we can make better decisions. To do that takes repetition so our brain and body find a new norm. One of the best ways to do this is meditation.

Step 1: Download an app, such as the Mindfulness Bell, or simply use the alarm function on your smartphone.

Step 2: Set the alarm to go off once an hour.

Step 3: Take 15 seconds to focus on listening and feeling yourself breathe.

The way our brain is designed, we cannot think when we focus on our breath. If we are big self-talkers or can't get our brain to shut off, this is an exercise we should attempt. On tough days, every 10 minutes I would take 15 seconds to focus.

Another activity: Take fifteen seconds to fix your gaze on one point and slowly take in all that you can really see. What did you see? Write down your thoughts in your journal or notebook, or on your computer.

I used to sit on my patio at night and watch the planes come in over South Mountain here in Phoenix, Arizona. It would probably take about a full minute for them to pass out of view. Over time, I was able to just go quiet in my head and allow my gaze to focus on the plane. We can also do these things with touch, smell, and taste.

Activity 6: Turn Around Your Fears

What if you could turn around your fears and go from complete fear to complete acceptance? I did it and you can, too. See my website, www.coachkennyweiss.com, to download the worksheet and learn how to do it.

Activity 7: Vision Board and Creating Your Manifesto

Chances are you've heard of vision boards, as they are quite popular for setting both personal and professional goals. But, I have a different twist on vision boards that will make all the difference in whether or not you succeed. See my website, www.coachkennyweiss.com, to download the worksheet.

Activity 8: Feelization

Directions:
1. Make a list of the best days or moments of your life. If you can't come up with any, grab your feelings list and pick a feeling like "safe" or "accomplished" and sit in it.
2. Spend as much time as possible each day feeling who you want to become. You can do this in the car, in a waiting room, or in the bathroom. This will help you to retrain your brain and body to release the

best day chemicals.

To access those feelings, you'll need to do a few simple things.
1. Determine what you want.
2. Imagine experiencing what you've set out to achieve.
3. Imagine how you'll feel when you've reached your goal.

Try to feel those feelings as much as possible. I'm not suggesting you need to spend several hours a day doing this but, instead of flipping through Facebook, spend a few minutes feeling what you want. You can do this even while sitting in your vehicle at a stoplight. Feel those feelings as much as possible. The best way to do that is to bring up something you have already experienced. It could be the day you got promoted. Sit in that feeling as much as possible or transfer that feeling into what it is you want to feel about a certain area of your life.

Activity 9: Shame Work

Directions: Make a choice not to shame yourself anymore and create a mantra. Whenever we talk down about ourselves it's a self-victimizing power grab. We are placing ourselves above God and above our own self-forgiveness.

We are re-victimizing ourselves to regain the power we lost in our original trauma. Make a choice and say, "No, I will not allow myself to talk about myself or my past decisions this way anymore." That is the choice. The mantra that I use is, "I did the best I could with what I knew at the time. Now that I know better, I do better."

What is your mantra?

Feelings like sadness, anger, shame, and frustration are good. Don't avoid them and give yourself permission to experience them. When you don't, you begin using them against yourself so that you can play the victim. This is a learning process. When my father was dying I felt tremendous moments of grief. More than thirty minutes of sitting in that grief would shut me down and I would head toward self-victimization. I would create moments or space to feel the grief but I limited that amount of time. I would follow that up with self-care activities or sit in front of my vision board feeling what I wanted in my life so that I could maintain a healthy balance.

Look at the areas where you are making yourself powerless. How do you give yourself away or manipulate others by doing things for them and expecting something in return? If you ever complain that you do things for others and they don't give back, most likely you are manipulating them and setting up your own self-victimization. This, again, reinforces the loss of power you experienced in your original trauma.

Ultimately, shame is all about control. We use our manipulations and self-victimization to control others. We overthink things. For instance, I discovered that while dating, because of my fear of abandonment, if I hadn't heard from someone I would obsessively think about some text I could send that didn't come off as needy but would get them to respond. Usually it was something nice. Being "nice" guilts people into responding and it is the single greatest way I see people self-victimize.

Our culture rightfully wants us to be kind to others, but in most cases we take that to the extreme. Most of us feel guilty or mean if we aren't nice. That is a huge red flag. Herein lies the problem: if they haven't been responding, they have already shown me they are not interested or maybe they are just busy. Instead of accepting that and being patient or moving on, I try to keep it going. The more I keep it going the more abandoned I feel. I am setting up my own self- victimization and trying to control them. Eventually, I would get angry and throw some big fit about how they were ignoring me. My anger and lack of acceptance then created a situation where they did not want to date me anymore. Voila, I had set up my own abandonment. I was in control of it. One thing to realize is that people never reject us. All they are ever doing is acting in their own best interest.

Activity 10: Just Say *No* Exercise

What would you say if I told you saying *no* is the most loving thing you can say to someone? I've shared my powerful story about learning to say *no* and would like to show you how to do it, too. The results will be life changing. See my website, www.coachkennyweiss.com, to download the worksheet.

Activity 11: Denial Work

Directions: Overcoming denial is about accepting that we did experience trauma and that the self-concept we developed to survive it isn't working for us. We are not bad or defective (if we think and feel that, we need to go back and do more shame work). None of us are; we just weren't aware. Becoming aware is our passport out of the Worst Day Cycle. Reading and learning are your ticket out of denial. See the following list of some of my recommendations for what to read and watch. We can only do what we know. If we aren't learning we can't do anything new.

Everything in our life is a result of our own choices. We are responsible for our own self- victimization. We set it up so no one does it to us. Until we admit this to ourselves and discover how we set this up, we cannot begin the process of learning how not to do it. We will be stuck in our pain and our darkness.

Denial is about three things:
1. The self-concept we developed to survive the trauma is most likely working against us and to let that go feels like the death of "us."
2. We go into denial because to succeed or step past that self-concept, we also have to let go of the person we became to keep our attachment to our parents or our perpetrator. If our trauma was from parenting, although we may logically know that what our parents did was less than nurturing, it is still our only attachment to them. To succeed, it would feel like we were dropping who we had to become to make them love us. So if we let go, we would feel completely alone in the world with no parents.
3. Anything we hate, judge, blame, or project is always about our denial of how we do those same things. These are pieces of ourselves we don't want to face. We are actually making an attempt to point those things out about ourselves. For instance, historically, Republicans have called Democrats a bunch of mamby-pamby emotional snowflakes. They use heavy emotions to describe a Democrat, which means they are also very emotional and don't like that about themselves. Democrats call Republicans racists and greedy, yet they want

to take everyone's money and use it as they see fit. If you voted for Donald Trump in the 2016 presidential election or have differing views, then you aren't allowed to speak. This has been happening all across college campuses and throughout the political season. That is racism. Both sides are talking about themselves as they project their personal denial onto the other side. Neither side is better or worse than the other.

Make a list of all the "problem" people and situations in your life and then ask: "What am I getting from the situation?" Saying you hate them or the setup or that you are getting nothing from it is denial and not true. These things are in your life because you get so much from them. Does it give you freedom, sympathy from others, lack of responsibility? Do others take care of everything for you? What is the payoff? What or whom are you afraid you would lose if you didn't have this "bad" situation in your life? Are you not ready to let it/them go?

Ask yourself the following:
- What would be the opposite view of this current situation?
- What has it cost me to not handle this? Am I willing to pay that cost?
- What could be the benefit of dealing with this?
- Six months from now, looking back on this situation, how would I have wanted myself to handle this situation?
- What if I got everything I wanted? What about that scares me?
- What if everything was just as it is supposed to be? How would I feel then?
- What if this current situation is setting me up for something even greater? What would it feel like if I let that in?

When I look over my life, don't I see that everything has always basically worked out? Wasn't there always something good that came out of each so-called "bad situation?"

The following are some things you can do to deal with your denial:
- Do mirror work daily, giving yourself permission to drop the old self-concept and welcome in your authentic self.

- Do mirror work daily, accepting that your caregivers loved you the best they could and would have done better had they known better. Remind yourself that by succeeding and moving past all of this, you will not be alone. Tell yourself that the most loving thing you can do for them and yourself is to move past this.
- Make a list of all the things you hate, judge, blame, criticize, and project and begin seeing how all of those items are operating in your life. You see them because they are you!

Hint: There is not always a direct correlation. For instance, someone who smokes pot may "hate" cigarette smokers. Well, they are also "smokers," just in a slightly different way. They are trying to talk to themselves when they make that judgment.

Be patient with yourself. It is going to take time for your brain and body to accept these new truths about yourself. Remember that it's a process, not perfection.

RESOURCES

Read:

Evolve Your Brain: The Science of Changing Your Mind by Joe Dispenza, HCI, Deerfield Beach, FL, 2008.

Another great book that gives you the science behind emotions, how illness drives them, and how our brain works against us when it comes to making change. This book taught me how feelings drive behaviors.

Facing Codependence: Where It is, Where It Comes From, How It Sabotages Our Lives by Pia Mellody, New York, NY, Harper & Row, 2003.

Facing Love Addiction: Giving Yourself the Power to Change the Way You Love by Pia Mellody, New York, NY, Harper & Row, 2003.

Loving What Is: Four Questions That Can Change Your Life by Byron Katie, Three Rivers Press, New York, NY, 2003.

This book will show you how to learn to deal with your denial. Our brain needs to reorient out of the shame and denial loop we are all in. Katie offers countless examples that will allow you to see yourself and your own shame and denial loop. This helps your brain get more comfortable with seeing reality so you can stop living in your Worst Day Cycle.

The Intimacy Factor: The Ground Rules for Overcoming the Obstacles of Truth, Respect and Lasting Love by Pia Mellody, New York, NY, Harper & Row, 2004.

All three of Pia Mellody's books should be mandatory reading for every young adult. They discuss the fundamentals of a healthy relationship, which none of us have been taught previously. My journey began with these books and I continually reread them to discover new nuggets of wisdom.

Molecules of Emotion: The Science Behind Mind-Body Medicine by Candace Pert, Simon & Schuster, New York, NY, 1999.

This book taught me the science of how we are all controlled by our emotions and not our thoughts. It was one of the books I read when I lost all of my clients.

***Parenting with Love and Logic* by Foster Cline and Jim Fay, NavPress Publishing, Colorado Springs, CO, 2006.**

This book taught me how to parent in a loving way without codependence and enmeshment. It puts the responsibility on our kids starting at a young age when their poor choices have very few real-life consequences. If you read this book, you will be amazed at how much easier it is to parent and how much your stress over being a parent will massively drop. This should be required reading for every new parent.

***The Body Keeps the Score: Brain, Mind and Body in Healing the Healing of Trauma* by Bessel van der Kolk, Penguin Books, London England, 2015.**

This book gave me a deeper understanding of how our body stores our trauma and why some sort of bodywork is essential to ending our Worst Day Cycle.

***The Power of Now: A Guide to Spiritual Enlightenment* by Eckhart Tolle, Namaste Publishing, Vancouver, Canada, 2004.**

This book helps with the *let it come* philosophy. Our brains need to shed some of their old neural pathways for this to make sense and seem possible. Get your brain familiar with the concepts and, over time, you will start seeing them just show up in your life. That will give you encouragement to keep going and start to understand the *let it come* philosophy more easily.

***You Can Heal Your Life* by Louise Hay, Hay House, Carlsbad, CA, 1984.**

In my opinion this is the single greatest book to learn how to build genuine self-esteem. You will also discover how you are using your emotions to make yourself sick and hurt. Hay's symptom list will give you a road map to unlock the feelings or trauma you are using to self-victimize.

WATCH:

Byron Katie's *He Won't Forget the Past* YouTube video: http://thework.com/en/resources/videos/he-wont-forget-past—-work-byron-katie-0

This video essentially changed my life. It shows what it looks like when we confront our self-victimization and denial and how by doing so, we free ourselves.

Dr. Nadine Burke Harris' How Childhood Trauma Affects Health Across a Lifetime TEDX talk: https://www.ted.com/talks/nadine_burke_harris_how_childhood_trauma_affects_health_across_a_lifetime?utm_campaign=tedspread--b&utm_medium=referral&utm_source=tedcomshare

This incredible TEDX talk by pediatrician Nadine Burke Harris backs up the ACE Study results. It illustrates how trauma is the leading cause of all of our maladies and is the reason we are all lacking the success and happiness we desire.

Dr. Robert Block on the Adverse Childhood Experiences (ACE) Study Go to YouTube and search for Dr. Robert Black

In this interview, Dr. Block, past president of the American Academy of Pediatrics, talks about the science behind the ACE Study and the impact it has on society.

Printed in Great Britain
by Amazon